S0-DOO-197

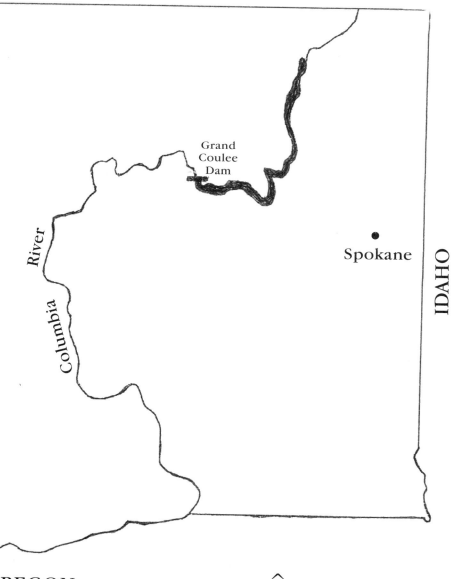

CANADA

Grand
Coulee
Dam

River

Columbia

• Spokane

IDAHO

OREGON

N

God's Marvels in Washington

Artists:
Anna and Sarah Turowski

Cover Artist:
Lester Miller

God's Marvels in Washington

in

Washington

Writer:
Anna L. Turowski

ROD AND STAFF PUBLISHERS, INC.
P.O. BOX 3, HWY 172
CROCKETT, KENTUCKY   41413
TELEPHONE (606) 522-4348

Copyright
1997
ROD AND STAFF PUBLISHERS, INC.
Crockett, Kentucky
41413
Printed in U.S.A.

ISBN 0-7399-0103-6
Catalog no. 2466

2   3   4   5   6   —   15   14   13   12   11   10   09   08   07   06

Grateful Acknowledgments:

To the Lord of all the earth, who does all things well and gives us richly all things to enjoy. Without Him this book would not have been possible.

To my father, who gave me many hands-on nature lessons and help in checking for accuracy.

To my mother, who sacrificed much so that her daughter could write, and who spent much time looking over the manuscript.

To my sister, Sarah, who offered suggestions and spent much time on her share of the artwork.

To my grandmothers and all others who gave encouragement and gladly lent resource materials. Without their help, this book would have been incomplete.

To the many sources I used to gather my information about the wonders of God's creation. Care has been taken to avoid direct quotations, but if there are any similarities found, I want to give credit to whom credit is due.

TABLE OF CONTENTS

Map Location:

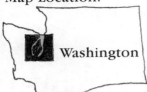
Washington

**STORY
AREA**

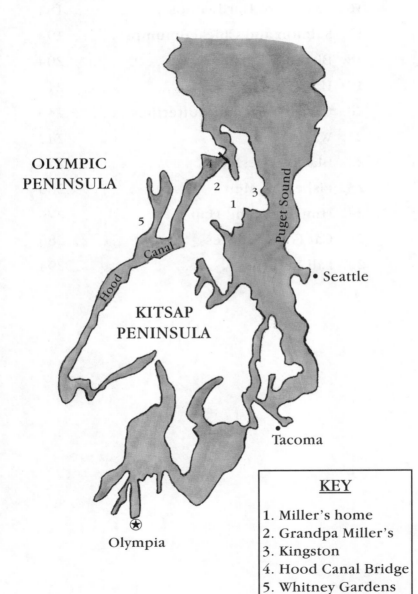

OLYMPIC
PENINSULA

Hood Canal

5

4

2

1

3

Puget Sound

• Seattle

KITSAP
PENINSULA

Tacoma

⊛
Olympia

KEY

1. Miller's home
2. Grandpa Miller's
3. Kingston
4. Hood Canal Bridge
5. Whitney Gardens

HOME AREA

Pussy Willows

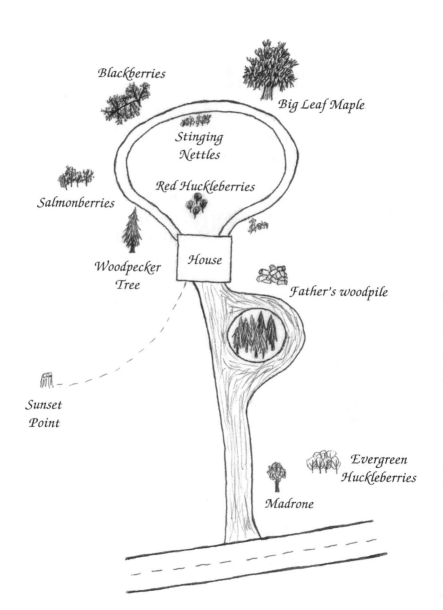

Blackberries

Big Leaf Maple

Stinging Nettles

Red Huckleberries

Salmonberries

Woodpecker Tree

House

Father's woodpile

Sunset Point

Evergreen Huckleberries

Madrone

Introduction

"Great and marvellous are thy works,
Lord God Almighty . . . "

The Lord created so many wonderful works
for us to enjoy! Each part of the world has its
own special beauty. Come and explore with
the Miller family the moist, picturesque, evergreen region where I was raised.

–*The Writer*

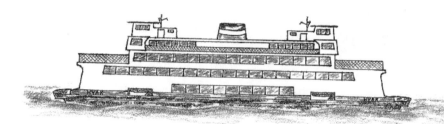

CHAPTER ONE

"The Lord is good unto them that wait for him, to the soul that seeketh him. It is good that a man should both hope and quietly wait for the salvation of the Lord."
Lamentations 3:25, 26

Welcome to Washington

"Oh, I can hardly wait!" exclaimed ten-year-old Ruth, glancing at the towering evergreens that were whipping past.

"Nor can I," Timothy replied with great enthusiasm.

"Grandpas! Grandpas! We're going to get Grandpas!" Four-year-old David bounced as far as his seat belt would allow.

Father smiled as he carefully steered around

14

a sharp corner. "It will be very good to see them again."

"Yes, it surely will." Mother nodded.

"I'm eager to hear Grandpa Kropf preach again," sixteen-year-old Joel put in. "I'm so glad the church asked him to help conduct this year's Bible conference."

"What ferry are we trying to catch?" Twelve-year-old Timothy glanced anxiously at the clock on the dashboard.

"I'd like to get the 10:10," Father answered.

"But it's 9:55 now!" Timothy frowned, flipping a stubborn lock of brown hair off his forehead. "We may not catch it."

"Then we would be late for meeting Grandpas at the airport." Ruth's blue eyes mirrored the concern in her voice.

"Well, children," Father replied calmly, "we will leave our times in the Lord's hands. I'm sure Grandpas will understand if we are late."

"Remember too," Mother said with a twinkle in her eyes. "Our heavenly Father runs the ferries."

A few minutes later, David's voice broke the silence. "I see it! I see the ferry!" he exclaimed at the sight of the big white boat that was nearing the dock.

"Oh, good," Timothy sighed in relief. "They haven't even docked yet."

Father pulled in beside one of the toll booths. "That will be $5.55 please." The man in the toll booth smiled at the eager group.

"Here you are," Father said, handing him the correct amount.

"Thank you." The man handed Father his receipt. "Proceed to Lane 7, please."

"Lane 7!" Timothy's shoulders slumped as Father pulled forward and drove down the designated lane. "We might not get this ferry after all!"

"Oh!" Ruth wailed. "What will we do?"

"We will trust the Lord, remember?" Father stopped behind a small blue truck and turned off the engine. "He is in control of all things and only allows what is best for us."

"And too," Joel said, scratching his head thoughtfully, "haven't we been in Lane 8 before and still caught the ferry?"

"You're right!" Timothy's eyes brightened. "The Lord must know that it is best for us to be at the airport on time."

"Lanes 5 and 6 are loading!" Ruth announced. "We're next!"

"It certainly doesn't pay to worry, does it,

children?" Father started the engine.

"No," Timothy admitted sheepishly. "I should have just trusted the Lord from the beginning."

Father joined the slow-moving ribbon of traffic that was boarding the ferry. "The Lord may not always see fit to bless our plans like this, children, but we can trust that He will always work things for our good."

"I'm thankful for that." Timothy nodded thoughtfully.

Ruth watched the cars ahead of them boarding the ferry. "I do hope we will park on the ramp. I enjoy being on the upper car deck."

Thump. Thump. The car left the dock and went down the loading ramp onto the ferry.

"Good! Oh, good!" David bounced in his seat. "That ferry man says we're supposed to go up the ramp! See him point?"

Father looked down at David. "Please don't get so excited, son. You must learn to be more patient."

David tried to sit still as they turned onto the side parking ramp. "We're going up, up, up!" He squirmed happily.

Joel shifted in his seat, getting a better view of the lane before them. "I'm surely glad I'm not driving, Father," he remarked. "It is a tight fit between those cars to our left and the side of the ferry."

"So it is," Father agreed, stopping behind the small truck once more. "I'm glad to be parked." He pushed in the parking brake. "They try to squeeze as many vehicles on a ferry as they can."

"How many cars can they fit on a ferry this size?" Ruth wondered.

Father answered, "This boat, the *Walla Walla*, is called a jumbo ferry. Jumbo ferries can hold two hundred cars and two thousand people."

"Oh!" Ruth glanced at all the cars crowded around them. "That's a lot!"

"May we go upstairs, Father?" Timothy asked, stretching his cramped arms. "I'd really like to watch from up there for a while."

"Certainly," Father consented. "I think we all would enjoy getting a little walk. We will be driving home through Tacoma instead of taking a ferry, so we'll want to stretch our legs now. I suppose you boys would like to go on the outer deck, wouldn't you?"

"We sure would." Joel and Timothy grinned at each other.

"Whoever is going out on that deck needs to take his coat," Mother told them. "That January wind is cold. And be sure that your ears are covered." She pulled David's cap snugly over his ears.

"All right," the children chorused, reaching for their coats.

Joel slipped out and held the door open for Ruth and Timothy. "Timothy," he warned, "don't push so hard on the door." He struggled to keep it from opening any farther. "You'll hit the car next to us."

"I forgot." Timothy stopped shoving and carefully slid out. "I guess I'm too eager to get upstairs."

Father took David's hand and led the way. "This is a crowded boat, so let's be sure to stay together." He raised his voice to be heard above the roar of the engine room.

They entered a doorway and climbed a flight of stairs. The roar of the engine was muffled as they stepped inside and the heavy metal door swung shut behind them. "Now," Father said, smiling, "who wants to go out on the front deck of the boat?"

"I do," the four children said in unison.

Mother smiled. "I will come too then, but

only for a few minutes. It can be rather cold out there."

"All right." Father turned and led them past the large windows and the bench seats that lined the inside of the ferry deck.

"Here we are," he announced, swinging open another heavy door that led them to the outer deck.

"Br-r-r-r-r!" David shivered as they went through a second door and stepped out into the biting wind. "It's cold—that wind is!" He huddled closer to Father.

"Ready to go back in already, son?" Father looked down at him.

"Y-y-e-e-es!" He shivered again. "Will you go in with me?"

"Well," Father replied, glancing at Joel's and Timothy's disappointed faces, "I think we'll stay out here a bit longer. Why don't you go back in with Mother? I think she is ready to go inside."

Mother smiled and shivered slightly. "Yes, I'm ready."

"Okay." David took Mother's hand. "Let's sit right by the door and wait, Mother. May we?"

"Yes," Mother agreed, guiding him through the door. "That will be just fine."

"And warmer too!" David grinned.

Leaning into the wind, Joel and Timothy headed for the front of the deck. "I need to hold onto my hat," Timothy said loudly, looking up at Joel. "If I don't, it just might disappear in Puget Sound!"

"I know what you mean!" Joel agreed, also raising his voice to be heard above the rushing roar of the wind. "Just don't take your hand off it!"

Soon Ruth and Father joined them. "I can see Seattle." Ruth leaned on the railing and looked at the sprawling metropolis ahead of them. "Soon we will see Grandpas!"

She shifted her gaze to the water below. "Oh, what is that?" she asked, pointing to the water near the boat.

"What?" Timothy hurried over to see.

"That clear thing down there—we're passing it now." She pointed. "Oh, now I can't see it anymore," she said disappointedly.

"Oh, but there's another one," she said eagerly a few moments later.

"I see it." Timothy looked over the rail at the umbrella-like form in the water below them. "That's a jellyfish, isn't it, Father?"

Father peered down into the water. "Yes,

21

you are right. That is a jellyfish. They are so interesting to watch."

"Yes," Ruth said, nodding. "But why are they called jellyfish?"

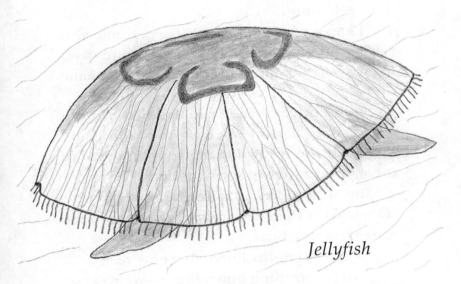

Jellyfish

"They feel almost like jelly," Father replied.

"I read somewhere that jellyfish are almost 96 percent water," Joel put in. "They would shrivel rather quickly if they were out of the water!"

"I would think so," Timothy agreed, still keeping a firm grip on his wind-whipped hat.

"Look." Ruth pointed toward the city, where

an odd-looking skyscraper towered amid other buildings. "You can see the Space Needle quite well now. Doesn't it remind you of a saucer on stilts?"

Father shifted his gaze to the ever-nearing city. "I didn't realize we were this close to Seattle already. You can see it well."

"Have you noticed Mount Rainier yet today?" Joel asked, motioning to a giant mountain in the distance. "It stands as a silent testimony to those in the busy city of the greatness of our Creator."

"How true," Father agreed, studying the huge snowcapped peak in the distance. "God's creation clearly declares His glory and power to all who will take the time to stop and observe its testimony."

"How high is Mount Rainier?" Ruth gazed in delight at the splendor of God's creation.

"It is 14,410 feet above sea level," Father answered. "It is the fourth highest mountain in the contiguous United States, which are the forty-eight states that border each other."

"Father," Joel said, looking over at him, "we are getting quite close to the dock."

"You are right." Father looked surprised. "We had better go back to the car right now.

*Ferry with Space Needle
and Mt. Rainier in background*

Thirty-five minutes can fly by so quickly."

Soon they left the ferry dock behind and entered the busy Seattle streets. "See how sharply those streets go uphill from the water," Ruth commented.

"I certainly wouldn't want to stop on one of those hills," Joel said, leaning over to get a better view. "But look at all those traffic lights. You would probably have to stop at least once."

"This is a busy city," Timothy remarked. "Many people going here and there and there and here."

"Seattle is Washington's largest city," Mother informed the children. "In 1990, it had a population of about 510,000 people, while Olympia, our state capital, only had about 33,000."

"That's quite a difference!" Timothy exclaimed, sitting up straighter.

Soon Timothy was glancing at the clock again. "Are we almost there, Father? Grandpa's flight will soon . . . " His voice trailed off. "Wait." He smiled and began again. "The Lord knows all about it, doesn't He?"

"That's right." Father grinned.

And before Timothy knew it, they had arrived at the Sea-Tac Airport.

"Here is the wing of the airport Grandpas will be coming to," Father announced when they were inside. "Now we need to find Gate 10. That is where they will be getting off the plane."

"There's Gate 10!" Joel saw it first. "A plane is pulling into it right now."

"I see it!" Timothy looked eagerly at the huge plane rolling slowly towards the building. "We made it in time." He heaved a sigh of relief. "God knew all about it."

"The passengers are unloading now," Ruth observed with excitement. "See them through the window on the walkway?"

"Yes, I saw Grandma!" David cried. He had been watching the little window too.

"Are you sure?" Timothy wondered. "I guess we'll soon find out. It is rather hard to see—"

"Grandpa! Grandma!" David interrupted him and rushed over to meet them.

"Welcome to Washington, Grandpa!" David squealed as he ran into Grandpa's arms.

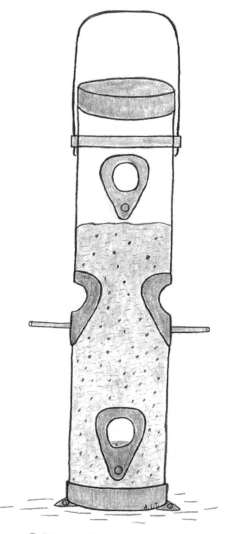

CHAPTER TWO

"Are not five sparrows sold for two farthings, and not one of them is forgotten before God? But even the very hairs of your head are all numbered. Fear not therefore: ye are of more value than many sparrows."

Luke 12:6, 7

Western Feathered Friends

"Tacoma surely is a busy place," Grandpa remarked, watching as Father carefully maneuvered through the surging lanes of traffic.

"Yes, it is," Father agreed, glancing over his shoulder to see if the right lane was clear. "It is one of the largest cities in the state." He signaled and moved into the right lane.

"Think of all the souls here," Grandpa said soberly. "Every one of them will spend eternity somewhere. And many are without God."

"That should inspire us to spread the Gospel light while we can," Father said, signaling and turning off onto the exit ramp that would take them to their home on the Kitsap Peninsula. "Jesus may return at any time, and then it will be too late. Their destiny will be sealed."

"Perhaps some of the people from the community will come to the Bible conference," Joel said hopefully. "That would be one way to reach souls. We put bulletins up around town."

"That is one of my prayers, Joel," Grandpa told him. "If the Lord can use these meetings in that way, may all the glory be His."

A few minutes later, David asked suddenly, "What is that big green thing up there, Father? Are we going to drive onto it?"

"Yes, David," Father replied. "Don't you remember driving over this bridge before? This is the Tacoma Narrows Bridge."

"That's an interesting name," Timothy said as they began the ascent onto the bridge. "Is it because the lanes are so narrow?" He eyed the four lanes critically with a mischievous grin playing on his face.

"No." Father chuckled softly. "This part of

Tacoma Narrows Bridge

the Puget Sound that we are crossing over is called the Tacoma Narrows."

"But the lanes do look narrow," Timothy said with a smile.

Another hour of driving brought them close to their destination. "Do you think it looks as though it will rain?" Grandma wondered, glancing up at the graying sky.

"That would not be unusual for around here," Father said, smiling. "Especially in the winter."

"Perhaps it will snow," Ruth said hopefully. "We don't often have snow."

"Then you might have to stay here longer, Grandma," Timothy teased.

"I'm afraid a little snow wouldn't keep us." She smiled back at Timothy. "We have a lot of snow back in Pennsylvania."

"That's true." Timothy grinned.

"I see our driveway! I see our driveway!" David cried out excitedly. "We're almost home!"

Father turned into the tree-lined drive. "Welcome to our home!" A short incline brought them into a clearing surrounded by huge conifer trees.

Grandpa looked at the modest home nestled in the clearing. "It's been a long time

Oregon race of dark-eyed junco

since we were here! How inviting it looks."

As soon as the car was unloaded, Mother and Grandma began preparing supper.

Ruth watched her bird feeder. "Mother, see how many birds are eating. I guess they know that it will soon be dark. They seem to be in a hurry to collect all the seeds they can."

"Maybe it will snow." Mother peered out the window at the cloud-covered sky. "The air is a bit nippy."

"What kind of birds are those?" Grandma joined Ruth at the window.

"Which ones?" Ruth wondered.

"The ones with black heads, white breasts, and brownish red backs. Their tails are black with white edges."

"Oh, those are juncos," Ruth answered. "We have quite a few of them coming to our feeders. I enjoy watching them flutter around and flick the white feathers on their tails."

"Those don't look like the juncos we have in Pennsylvania," Grandma commented. "Their tails are somewhat the same, but ours are mostly gray with creamy, white breasts."

Ruth went to get her bird book. "See?" She flipped to the page with the juncos. "I believe that we have the Oregon race of dark-eyed

Western rufous-sided towhee

juncos and you have the slate-colored race."

"Oh, yes." Grandma carefully studied the pictures in the book. "That is interesting. I didn't realize that God made so many varieties of juncos." She looked again at the pretty little birds gathering what seeds they could before darkness enveloped the forest.

Suddenly a black, rust, and white form hopped out of the bushes and flapped up to the deck. "Now he looks familiar." Grandma smiled as the red-eyed bird sent seeds flying in his hasty landing. He busied himself with scratching for the seeds that had fallen out of the feeder on the railing above him. "That is a rufous-sided towhee, if I don't miss my guess."

"You're right." Ruth watched him hop about. "But he is a western rufous-sided towhee. Can you guess what the difference between eastern and western is?"

"Three thousand miles!" Timothy piped up.

"No," Ruth said, turning to smile at her brother.

"Let's see." Grandma studied the robin-sized bird carefully. "He has white splotches on his back. Is that the difference?"

"That's exactly what I was thinking of." Ruth confirmed her guess as the towhee sent seed hulls flying in his quick descent to the ground.

"What other visitors do you have that I wouldn't know?" Grandma wondered.

"There are the varied thrushes," Ruth told her. "They nearly look like robins. They aren't as tame as the smaller birds that visit our feeder, but they are quite beautiful."

"I would enjoy seeing a varied thrush," Grandma told her.

"Oh, look, there's one now!" Ruth exclaimed. "He's across the lawn on that feeder hanging from the storage shed."

Varied thrush

"Oh, yes." Grandma spotted the orange-and-black bird. "Is there a difference between the male and the female? I see one below the feeder whose breast stripe doesn't look quite as black."

"Then that must be a female," Ruth replied. "Females have a gray breast stripe instead of a black one."

"The Lord has made so many interesting birds," Grandma said. "It has been a pleasure to learn about a few more of them."

CHAPTER THREE

"Come now, and let us reason together, saith the Lord: though your sins be as scarlet, they shall be as white as snow; though they be red like crimson, they shall be as wool."

Isaiah 1:18

Snow Fun

After supper, David hurried to the window. "Oh! Oh! Look! It must be snowing! Look at all those white cotton balls falling from the sky!" He watched as the huge, wet flakes floated down through the beams of the outdoor light.

"You're right!" Timothy and Ruth rushed to join him, the others following at a slower pace.

"It is so beautiful." Mother admired the large flakes drifting softly out of the sky.

"Yes," Grandpa agreed. "The freshly falling snow always reminds me of the cleansing power of Jesus' blood. God has promised to make our hearts as white as snow when we come to Him for cleansing."

"The ground is even white, and it's getting deeper," Timothy remarked. "I'm going to measure it!" He hurried to the closet to get the yardstick.

"I'll come too." Joel was right behind him.

"You can tell we don't have much snow." Father smiled at the eager children. "Usually, we have it once or twice a year."

"I had thought that being this far north, you would have more snow," Grandpa said thoughtfully. "But it must be because the Pacific Ocean and several smaller bodies of water are not far away that the temperature doesn't drop so much in the winter."

"I think that is right," Father agreed.

"Just what *is* snow?" Ruth wondered.

"Snow is tiny ice crystals," Mother explained. "But no two snowflakes are exactly alike. God gave each one its own special design."

"That's hard to imagine." Timothy had come back inside. "The Lord's wisdom is far above mine!" He swung the yardstick for emphasis. "Oh!" He suddenly remembered why he had the yardstick in his hand. "I forgot to tell you right away. We have half an inch already! If this keeps up, we might have five whole inches!"

"Then we can make a snow house!" Ruth exclaimed excitedly.

Timothy hurried into the kitchen from the outdoors the next morning. "There are six inches out there!" He rubbed his frigid hands together. "It added some excitement to my chores."

Mother looked outside at the graceful ever-green branches bent under their heavy coat of snow. "I would think so!" she replied, expertly flipping a golden pancake.

Grandma smiled. "It is obvious that you are not used to a lot of snow, Timothy. If you lived back in Pennsylvania, you would often have snow to add to your choring excitement."

"I marked a place for a snow house," Joel said. He stomped the snow off his boots at the back door.

"Good," Ruth said happily. "When do we start?"

Mother laughed. "Not until after breakfast. You should get some warm food in your stomachs first."

42

Snow house

"Of course." Joel smiled, rubbing his empty stomach. "I wouldn't want to miss pancakes."

Mother slid a stack of steaming pancakes onto the platter in the oven. "You may play outside this morning, but I'd like your help in the afternoon. We will have plenty to do with the Bible conference starting tomorrow."

After breakfast, the children busily packed snow into dishpan "molds" and stacked their bricks into walls. "Let's put a window here." Timothy puffed as he set another block onto the wall. "That will make fewer blocks to pack!"

43

"Better yet, let's make two or three windows. Do you agree, Ruth?" Joel set his brick next to Timothy's.

"That's fine," Ruth declared.

"Snow! Snow!" David threw handfuls of wet, fluffy flakes into the air. "I'll help you pack that brick, Joel!" He ran toward Joel as fast as he could in the mass of slippery whiteness.

"Whee-e-e!" He slipped and landed gently on his back. He lay very still.

"Are you all right?" Joel rushed over and looked down at a silent David.

"Yes." David lay stiffly in his snow bed. "I just like to lay in the snow. It feels good!"

"Okay." Joel grinned down at him. "Have a good time."

"I will." David began to roll over and over.

"Now you look like a snowman," Timothy teased, eyeing his snow-covered brother.

"I'm no 'nowman," David sputtered through the snow on his face. "I'm a 'nowboy!"

"I see," Timothy replied, laughing. "A snow boy you are!"

"David! David!" Mother called from the open doorway. "You had better come in and warm yourself. You will get too cold with all that snow on your face."

"All right, Mother," he replied. "But may I look at these funny holes first?"

"If you are quick," she consented. "Then hurry in."

"What funny holes?" Ruth came over to see.

"Those." David pointed to a trail of animal tracks in the snow.

"Br-r-r-r." He suddenly shivered. "I'm going inside. But tell me what made those holes. I want to know." He rushed into the house to get warm.

"What made these tracks, Joel?" Ruth asked as he approached.

"They look like rabbit tracks to me," he replied. "I didn't realize we had wild rabbits around here. Why don't we join David inside and see what we can find out about our visitor. Maybe we can finish the snow house later. My fingers are getting too cold." He rubbed his gloved hands together rapidly.

"I can't figure this out," he said, looking up from a field guide a few minutes later. "Of all the books we've looked in, the only rabbit or hare we have here is the snowshoe hare."

"And Mother said the only rabbits she has seen have been brown in the winter," Ruth put in. "Snowshoe hares are white in the winter."

Snowshoe hare

"I wonder if there would be anything in this book." Timothy pulled a large Audubon book off the shelf. He soon found the rabbit and hare section.

"Listen to this!" he suddenly exclaimed. "It says that the snowshoe hare doesn't change color in the humid lowlands of Washington and Oregon!"

"Really?" Joel took the book and found where Timothy had been reading. "You are right." He smiled. "The rabbit—actually, hare—mystery has been solved. I had no idea we had the snowshoe hare around here."

"This Golden guide says that the snowshoe hare has relatively short ears," Ruth commented. "That explains why Mother thought she had seen a rabbit instead of a hare. Usually hares have longer ears than rabbits."

"I'm glad that you looked in that book, Timothy," Joel told him. "Won't Mother be surprised when she finds out what the 'rabbit' really was?"

"Yes. And we must tell David too. I'm glad he found those tracks."

CHAPTER FOUR

"In every thing give thanks: for this is the will of God in Christ Jesus concerning you."
1 Thessalonians 5:18

Rain, Rain, Rain

"Rain. Rain. Rain. And Grandpas have gone, and the snow is gone," David said drearily as he sat by the window. "Rain. Rain." The tiny drops pitter-pattered on the front deck. "Rain," he sighed, walking to another window and watching it splash in the puddles on the back lawn. "Rain, rain, rain."

"Why so glum?" Joel asked him. "Aren't you glad that God sends the rain?"

David shrugged his shoulders.
"I don't know. I wanted to play
outside with Sparkie this afternoon. Now he is all wet. His fur
isn't nice and soft when he is wet.
Just look at him. He isn't even in
his doghouse where he would stay dry!"

Joel smiled. "Maybe Sparkie likes the rain."
He watched Sparkie splash through a puddle

behind Timothy, who was carrying a bowl of scraps out to the chickens.

"How come Timothy gets to be outside and I don't?" David whined.

"David." Mother came into the room. "What happened to my happy boy? He seems so gloomy this afternoon." She stroked his curly brown hair.

"I want to be outside, but it is raining. And Sparkie is too wet and Timothy is outside and . . . and . . ." Tears started trickling down his cheeks.

"Now just a minute." Mother sat him on her lap. "You must stop crying and be a happy boy again. We can't always do everything that we want to do. God has a good reason for sending rain. So we shouldn't complain, should we?" Mother asked softly.

"No." David shook his head. "I will try to be happy, Mother, but I miss grandpas too."

"I know." Mother stroked his curly hair. "But Grandpas needed to go back home. Grandpa has much work to do for the Lord there. We should be thankful he and Grandma could come, even if it was only for a short time. The Lord used the meetings here to help a number of people, and now Grandpa has more people to tell about the Lord Jesus back at his home. So can you be a thankful boy?"

David nodded. "I am thankful Grandpa and Grandma could come."

"That sounds much better." Mother smiled at him. "Shall we make some cookies now? That is a good thing to do on a rainy day."

"Yes." David brightened. "I'd like that."

"So would I." Joel grinned. "It would be my pleasure to help . . . eat them, that is!"

"Eat what?" Timothy entered the house, dripping wet.

"Cookies!" David replied excitedly as he slid from Mother's lap.

"Oh, good." Timothy took off his rain hat. "Then I'd be happy to help eat them too."

"I'd like to help make them," Ruth said as she entered the room.

"How do you know what we are talking about?" Joel teased. "You don't like to make . . . let me think . . . make . . . " He paused.

"Cookies," Ruth finished for him.

"But you said that you like to make cookies," Timothy joined in. "Now you don't?"

"No. No." Ruth smiled. "I meant that you're making cookies, and I *do* like to make them. I could hear you talking all the way upstairs in my bedroom!"

"Oh," Timothy said with a grin, pulling off his jacket. "I see."

"Wet out there?" Joel asked, stepping backwards to avoid the puddle Timothy's dripping clothing made on the floor.

"Yes, it is," Timothy answered. "Mother, why does it rain so much here? We seem to have more than our share of rain." He hung his coat on the rack and reached for an old towel to wipe up the puddle he had brought in.

"Well," Mother said, pulling her recipe for gingerbread cookies out of the recipe box, "partly because we live near the Pacific Ocean."

"What makes it rain, Mother?" Ruth asked. "Please tell us that before you tell us why we get so much."

"That is difficult to explain." Mother thought for a moment. "Do you know what gravity is? Gravity is a force or power that causes things to move toward the earth. It is what makes a pencil fall to the floor if you drop it. God made gravity so we can stay on the ground. Without it, we would just float around."

"That would be fun," Ruth said.

"Not for long," Joel told her. "You couldn't

sit down unless you held yourself to your chair, and the cookie dough would be floating around in the air, if you could even get it mixed!"

"Is that word g-g—?" David began.

"Grav-i-ty," Joel supplied.

"Gravity," Ruth repeated. "What does gravity have to do with rain, Mother?"

"Gravity is what pulls the rain to the earth," Mother began again. "Every cloud is made of tiny water droplets or ice crystals. At first the water droplets are very small—too small to fall. The droplets increase in size for a couple different reasons. One reason is that they collide and merge as they are blown around in the cloud. They join together and get bigger and bigger until they are too heavy to stay in the air any longer. Gravity then causes them to fall to the ground.

"A second way," Mother went on, "is for some tiny water droplets and ice crystals to be in the same cloud. The water droplets evaporate, or change into a vapor (like steam from a teakettle). That vapor gathers on the ice crystals. The crystals grow larger and larger and eventually fall to the earth. Sometimes they come as snow, and other times they melt into rain as they pass through the warm air."

"That's amazing!" Timothy tried to grasp it all. "I didn't know all that had to happen just for it to rain! We certainly have a great Creator. He made everything work just right."

"This reminds me of some verses in the Book of Job," Joel said. He paged through his Bible. "Here they are, in chapter 36. 'Behold, God is great . . . For he maketh small the drops of water: they pour down rain according to the vapour thereof: which the clouds do drop and distil upon man abundantly.'"

Mother smiled. "Those verses describe it very well. Right in the Bible, we have a perfect description of how rain is made.

"Now for your question, Timothy. Why do we have an abundance of rain? Here in the Pacific Northwest, the wind almost always blows from the west. This brings all the clouds and storms from the Pacific Ocean. As the warm air from the Pacific Ocean comes toward the land, it has to rise and cross over the Olympic Mountains near our coast. As the warm air goes up over the mountains, it gets cooler. Because cold air can't hold as much moisture, it begins to rain. They get much more rain on the west side of those mountains than we do here on the east side. We live in between two sets of mountains. The Olympics are to the west and the Cascades are to the east."

"Then Mount Rainier is part of the Cascade Mountain range, isn't it?" Timothy wondered.

"That's correct," Mother answered. "The air gets colder again as the clouds go up over the Cascades, and they lose even more rain. That falls on our area here. We get thirty to sixty inches of rain a year."

Joel had gone to get his old textbook on the Pacific Northwest. "It says in here that we have rain at least 150 to 210 days a year. Moisture is plentiful. Our climate, or average weather, is mild, not too hot and not too cold. That's because we live so close to the Pacific Ocean and the warm water current that moves through it. Our winters aren't usually very cold. The temperature rarely drops below zero."

"Not like at Grandpa's!" Ruth said.

"It rarely goes above ninety degrees in the summer either," Mother put in. "But summer does bring more sunshine than the wintertime, doesn't it, David?"

"Yes," David answered brightly. "Then Sparkie and I can play."

"This is February now," Mother told him. "In three or four more months, we should have lots of sunshine."

"I actually like the rain," Joel said, watching it streak past the window. "Because God gives us so much rain, our region stays green all year round. That is also why our trees are so tall."

David smiled. "I think I will like rain too. Maybe it will make Sparkie clean. He needed a bath anyway!"

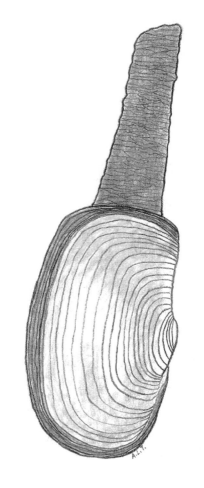

CHAPTER FIVE

"Let the heaven and earth praise him, the seas, and every thing that moveth therein."

Psalm 69:34

"Mr. Tie"?

"Tim-o-o-thy! Ru-uth!" David called excitedly one afternoon. "We're go-o-ing to Grandfather's! We're go-o-ing to Grandfather's! Come quickly!"

Timothy bounded up the back deck steps with Ruth right behind. "What for?" he panted.

David scratched his head. "I think Mother said that Mr. Tie has gone out to see Grandfather Millers."

"Mr. Tie?" Ruth looked puzzled. "I'm going to ask Mother who he is." She determinedly opened the back door.

"Mother," she called, "who is Mr. Tie, and what is he doing at Grandfather's?"

Mother looked up from the plate of cookies she was wrapping. "What did you say? Mr. Tie at Grandfather's?"

"That's what David said," Timothy affirmed. "Mr. Tie has gone out to see Grandfather."

"Oh, now I know." Mother smiled. "The tide is out on Grandfather's beach. It's one of the lowest tides of the year, and he wants us to come and explore the beach."

"Oh." Timothy grinned, flipping his stubborn brown lock off his forehead. "If that is what Mr. Tie is, I'd like to go see him right now."

"What is Mr. Tie?" David asked, puzzled, as they began the short drive to Grandfather's. He had not been able to follow the others' conversation.

"Well, David," Mother began, "he, or rather, it, is really a tide, not Mr. Tie. A tide is the rise and fall of the ocean's surface."

David wrinkled his brow. "Does Grandfather live along the ocean then?"

"No," Mother explained. "Grandfather lives

along the Hood Canal. It is connected to the ocean, but the ocean is much bigger."

"Oh," David replied, scratching his head.

"You'll understand it better when you get big like Timothy." Mother patted his arm.

"Okay." He smiled happily.

"But why does the ocean rise and fall?" Ruth wondered.

"The gravity of the moon is the main reason for the tides," Mother answered as she turned into Grandfather's lane. "The moon's gravity is the pull of the moon, just like the earth has gravity."

"And the gravity of the earth—that's what pulls the rain down, isn't it?" Ruth commented.

"Yes, it is. The gravity of the moon pulls the sea water on the earth slightly to one side or the other as the earth turns around. There are two high tides and two low tides in each twenty-four-hour day."

"Isn't the tide later each day?" Timothy asked.

"Yes," Mother replied, skillfully parking at the end of the lane. "The moon rises later each day, and so it pulls the tide in later each day too. High tides are about fifty minutes later every day."

"In between the two high tides is a low, or ebb, tide," Timothy told Ruth. "That's what we're going to see—a very low tide." He opened the car door and headed for the house.

Soon Timothy and Ruth were running up and down the beach. Mother and David followed more slowly with Grandfather and Grandmother. Small treed hills lined the opposite shore of the canal, and the majestic Olympic Mountain range rose behind them in the distance.

"Ee-ee-k!" Ruth suddenly squealed. "Water came out of that hole and squirted me!"

"Was that all?" Timothy teased. "Why, that's nothing to get upset about." He hurried over. "It was just a—o-oh!" He jumped. "I got squirted in the face!"

Ruth giggled. "Now its friend got you."

Timothy grinned sheepishly. "I guess," he admitted. "I'll have to be careful around here." He advanced more cautiously.

"What got Timothy?" David asked worriedly.

Mother smiled. "Timothy is fine. It was only a clam that squirted him."

"Tell us more about clams please, Grandfather." Ruth walked over to him, avoiding the holes in the sand.

Timothy being squirted by a clam

"Clams are mollusks," Grandfather began. "Mollusks are soft-bodied animals that are usually covered with a hard shell."

Timothy picked up an old clamshell that was lying on the beach. "Grandfather, what holds these two pieces of the shell together so tightly when a clam is inside?"

"Clams have powerful muscles that hold the shell shut," Grandfather answered.

Grandmother asked with a smile, "Did you know that God gave clams a foot?"

"A foot?" Ruth glanced mischievously at her own two feet.

"Yes." Grandmother nodded. "But not like yours. God gave them a hatchet-shaped muscle that we call a foot. The clam uses his foot for digging into the sand or mud."

"How?" Ruth wondered.

"He sticks his foot into the sand," Grandmother explained. "The tip is expanded to grip the sand, and it pulls the clam downward. So they do use their feet to move!"

"But why did they squirt Timothy and Ruth?" David wondered. "That wasn't kind!"

"Clams have two hollow tubes," Grandfather tried to explain. "They use one tube to take in water that has their food, which is tiny plants and animals, in it. The other tube is for expelling the used water. When they are disturbed by someone walking nearby, they sometimes squirt out that water."

"So he used his 'used water' to squirt me?" Timothy grinned.

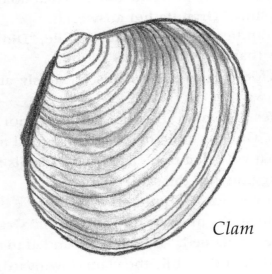

Clam

"I suppose." Grandfather grinned back.

Meanwhile, David had been wandering down the beach. "Grandfather, come quickly!" he suddenly cried. "Please tell me what this funny thing is." He poked at a red-orange wrinkled mass sticking out of the sand. "Hurry, please, Grandfather, it's going away!"

Grandfather quickly walked over to the small boy.

"Oh," David sighed. "It disappeared. It was so funny, Grandfather. It was all wrinkly. But now you can't tell me what it was!"

"I think I can without seeing it," Grandfather assured him. "See the big hole in the sand that it left? It must have been a geoduck."

"A what?" Timothy had joined them. "A gooey duck?"

"Yes." Grandfather smiled. "A geoduck. It's the largest of our burrowing clams. Its name is spelled *g-e-o-d-u-c-k*, but you pronounce it *gooey* duck."

"Does it look like a duck?" David wondered.

"No," Grandfather told him. "It looks like a great big clam. Once someone found one that weighed almost sixteen pounds!"

"O-o-oh! That was a large clam!" Ruth exclaimed.

"They live in burrows three feet from the surface of the sand," Mother added. "And they keep their long necks at the top of the sand. That was what David saw."

"Yes." Grandfather looked down at the hole

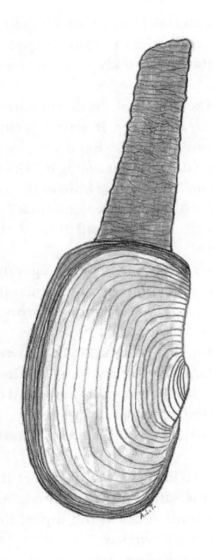

Geoduck

again. "When geoducks are disturbed, they take their necks down into their burrows. But they can't ever fit all of their neck into their shell with them. Their necks are so big that they can only pull them in part way!"

"Can you eat them?" Timothy wondered.

"They have red orange flesh." Grandfather looked straight at him with a twinkle in his eye. "Would you want to?"

Timothy shrugged his shoulders. "If they taste good."

Grandfather smiled. "Yes, they are edible. They are quite popular and considered a delicacy clam with some people."

"You'd eat one if I fixed it for you," Mother told him.

"Of course," Timothy replied. "I'm thankful for anything you cook, and if I don't care for it, well—I'll eat it anyway!"

"What was it called again?" David asked.

"A geoduck," Grandmother answered.

"Gooey duck," David repeated, starting down the beach.

"Here's another!" He pointed. "And another! Goo-oo-ey duck! Goo-oo-ey duck!" He ran across the beach, dodging squirting clams.

CHAPTER SIX

"And they [Israel] shall spring up as among the grass, as willows by the water courses."

Isaiah 44:4

Kittens and Beavers

"Guess what it's time for?" Father asked after the morning chores were done one Saturday.

"Is it time for my nap?" David whispered in disappointment.

"No." Father smiled at him. "It is still morning. You take naps in the afternoons."

"Oh, good!" he exclaimed in relief.

"I wouldn't know what it's time for." Timothy shrugged his shoulders.

"It's time to gather some pussy willows. February is when the buds open. Mother would like some to put in a vase. I thought you all would enjoy going on a walk with me."

"I would like that," Ruth told him.

"I thought you would," Father replied with a smile. "I know just the spot to get some pussy willows."

"May I come too?" David asked.

"Yes, you may," Father said. "Go and get your coats, children. The air is still a bit nippy."

"This is fun." Timothy pushed his way through the salal bush a few minutes later. "You know what, Ruth? We should play hide-and-seek back here with all this salal around." He tugged at a leathery, fine-toothed leaf. "Even Joel could easily hide in this thicket. Some of it is six feet tall!"

"Maybe we can do that this afternoon after the cleaning is done," Ruth said, plucking off a shiny dark-green leaf from a salal she was walking by. "How much farther is it, Father?" She glanced at the dull, pale underside before dropping the leaf.

"Just a little farther," he replied as he helped David through the rigid branches of another salal.

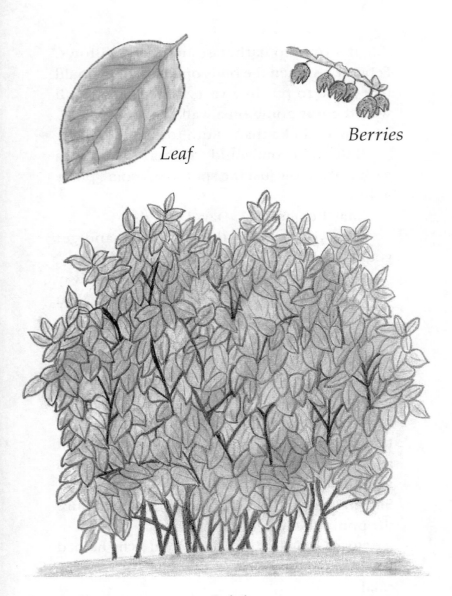

Leaf

Berries

Salal

"Whoa!" Timothy's foot sank into a hole. "Watch out, Ruth. Here's a mountain beaver's hole. I forgot to watch for them!"

Ruth carefully stepped over the hole. "Oh." Her foot sank into the soft dirt next to the hole. "Now why did that happen?" She pulled out her dirt-covered shoe. "I stepped around the hole, and I still sank in."

"Mountain beavers' tunnels are shallow and often collapse," Father told her. "Especially when girls step on them."

"I see." Ruth smiled. "Do they collapse for fathers too?"

"Why, of course." He laughed.

"I know all about mountain beaver holes," Timothy emphasized. "But I don't know much about the hole diggers. They aren't really beavers, are they?"

"No." Father helped David over another hole. "They are really a rodent one foot to a foot and a half long with a small, short tail. They only mountaineer occasionally! Perhaps their habit of eating bark and twigs earned them the name beaver."

"What else do they eat?" Ruth wondered.

"Well," Father began, "they also eat ferns, leaves, stems, and roots. God has given them

Mountain beaver

the ability to climb trees, but they can only go about twenty feet up. They climb Douglas fir trees and clip off the twigs for food. They also make hay by laying piles of plants on logs to dry them for winter storage."

"What interesting creatures! But why haven't I ever seen one?" Timothy wondered. "We have enough holes around here."

"They are nocturnal, or active at night," Father explained. "They are also active on autumn days, but they are solitary creatures and probably hide when they—whoa!" Father's foot went down into a hole.

Ruth grinned. "They do catch fathers."

Father chuckled. "Yes. I should watch where I'm going! Those little beavers have lots of tunnels."

After they had traveled another few hundred feet, Father announced, "Here we are." The small grove of willows contrasted with the evergreens surrounding it.

"Oh, look at all those kitty trees!" David ran over and tried in vain to reach a branch. He turned imploringly to Father. "Will you get me one please?"

"Certainly," Father said, opening his pocket-knife and cutting off a small twig for him.

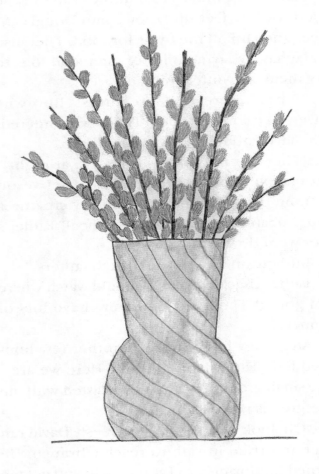

Pussy willows

"Here, Ruth." He handed her several more he had cut.

"What are pussy willows, anyway?" Ruth wondered.

"They are the willow's flowers." Father handed her a branch from another tree. "God made pussy willows dioecious, which means one tree has male flowers and another has female flowers. As the flowers grow larger, the female's will turn a silver green and the male's a golden yellow. When ours are bigger, we will be able to tell what they are."

Ruth stroked a soft silver catkin. "It feels just like a kitten."

"Yes. Yes." David rubbed his vigorously.

"Be careful, David," Timothy warned. "Or your kitty won't have any fur left!"

"Well, well," Mother greeted them as they entered the house with their brown-and-gray bouquets. "Thank you very much."

She glanced down at their feet. "What happened to you? You look as though your shoes had a dirt bath!"

"They did," Timothy replied with a grin, "thanks to the seldom-mountaineering non-beaver!"

CHAPTER SEVEN

"The glory of Lebanon shall come unto thee, the fir tree . . . to beautify the place of my sanctuary; and I will make the place of my feet glorious."

Isaiah 60:13

Monarch of the Washington Forest

"Father," Ruth and Timothy began as they approached him one afternoon in early March, "Joel said that you could give us some lessons in tree identification."

"I would be glad to." Father smiled from his seat on a cedar stump. "What do you want to know?" He skillfully brought his hatchet down on a piece of cedar wood.

"We would like to be able to tell the

different types of trees apart." Timothy spoke for the pair.

"I'll do my best," Father said, taking the thin sticks of kindling he had chopped and placing them in a pile. "When I was a boy, your great-uncle Elmer gave me many lessons about the wonders of God's creation."

Timothy flipped his stubborn lock off his forehead. "What happened to Uncle Elmer, Father? I think you have mentioned him before."

A shadow of sadness drifted over Father's face. "He is Grandfather Miller's brother, you know," he said. "When Joel was just a baby, Uncle Elmer's wife, Jewel, passed away. He became bitter toward the Lord and left the church. Today he lives a lonely life near the coast of Washington."

"May we visit him someday?" Ruth wondered. "I want to meet him."

Father stroked his chin thoughtfully. "I would really like to, Ruth. I have been praying for him for many years. Each time Grandfather writes to him, Uncle Elmer doesn't want us to come for a visit. We can keep praying for him. Perhaps he will want us to visit him soon."

They stood silently for a few minutes, each

busy with his own thoughts.

Timothy broke the silence first. "Will you please tell us about this tree now, Father?" He leaned over and touched the reddish gray brown bark of a tall tree. "Perhaps you can tell us what Uncle Elmer told you."

Father nodded. "That is a Douglas fir," he said. "Douglas firs are the second tallest trees in America. Only the trees from the sequoia family are larger."

"How tall do Douglas fir trees grow?" Ruth wondered, looking up at the giant tree towering well over one hundred feet above her.

"They are usually 150 to 230 feet tall." Father rolled another piece of cedar wood over to split. "In the rain forests along our coast, they can be up to 325 feet tall. One was recorded as being 380 feet tall and 15 feet in diameter!"

"Now that is tall!" Timothy exclaimed.

Spotting a Douglas fir branch that had fallen in a windstorm, Father bent over and picked it up. "Notice that the needles are all about three-quarters of an inch long. They point out from the twig in all directions, just like bottlebrush bristles."

Ruth reached out to feel the flat yellow

Douglas Fir

green needles. "The ends aren't very sharp," she remarked. "But they are pointed."

"I also want you to study the bark," Father said. "Bark is important in tree identification. See the deep reddish grooves running up and down the tree? They separate the gray brown ridges in the bark. It reminds me somewhat of fried bacon. I remember Uncle Elmer telling me that too.

"The Douglas fir is not really a true fir," Father went on. "God made Douglas fir tree cones to hang down from the branches, while true fir cones stand upright on their branches."

"How did it get its name then?" Timothy wondered.

"It was named Douglas after the botanist who studied it," Father replied. "He determined that it was not related to any of the known conifers. It is called Douglas fir to keep it from being identified with the other classes of trees."

Pee-oo! Pee-oo! A shrill voice interrupted Father. All heads turned in the direction of the noisemaker.

"A Douglas squirrel," Father said softly. "He is on that branch about twenty feet up."

"The brown-and-gray squirrel with his rusty orange belly nervously twitched his tail as he

Douglas squirrel

scooted to a higher branch. *Pee-oo! Pee-oo!* He sat up very straight and started eating seeds from a cone he had fetched from one of his nearby stockpiles.

"He certainly eats in a hurry." Timothy watched as the squirrel made a quick end of his meal and dropped the remains on the ground below. Timothy quietly walked over and picked up the piece he had dropped.

Pee-oo! The squirrel darted up the tree.

"You didn't leave much of a cone for us to study!" Timothy called after him, holding the remains of the cone up toward the scampering creature.

"Douglas squirrels really enjoy conifer seeds," Father said, straining for a last glance at the retreating figure. Shifting his gaze, he scanned the ground for a fallen cone. "Here is one that is somewhat better for studying." He picked up an old, dry cone that had lost all of its seeds. "Douglas fir tree cones are usually three to four inches long. See the thin, rounded scales. And notice these three-forked 'tongues' sticking out from between the scales. They are called bracts and are one of the characteristic features of Douglas fir cones."

Timothy took the cone and felt the little bracts. "They almost feel like the popcorn hulls that get stuck in my teeth."

"Yes." Father smiled. "That is one way to put it.

"Did you know that the Douglas fir is one of the most valuable lumber trees?" Father asked them. "Two-thirds of the lumber cut in the Pacific Northwest is Douglas fir. The hard, strong wood is almost free of knots. That makes excellent wood for boards. Can you think of something else necessary for board lumber, Timothy?"

Timothy eyed the tall giants around him. "A straight trunk, perhaps?"

"That was what I had in mind," Father told him. "Now, Ruth, after our lesson, can you find a piece of Douglas fir in this stack of wood I have left to split?"

"Here is one, I am sure," Ruth announced, after studying the pieces for a moment. "I can tell by the bark."

"Good," Father praised her. "Douglas fir is one of the better trees for firewood in this area, but madrone and big leaf maple are better than the Douglas fir."

"Will you tell us about them?" Ruth wondered.

Father picked up his stack of kindling. "Let's save them for another day. Class is ended for now." He smiled as they walked to the house together.

CHAPTER EIGHT

*"Consider the lilies of the
field, how they grow; they toil
not, neither do they spin: and
yet I say unto you, that even
Solomon in all his glory was
not arrayed like one of these."*
Matthew 6:28, 29

Spring Surprise

"Mother, may we go for a walk?" Ruth asked one afternoon in mid-March. "It's such a beautiful springlike day! David and I would like to see if there are any flowers blooming yet."

Mother looked up from the bread she was shaping into loaves. "That sounds like a good idea. Let me finish with this dough, and I will go with you. Perhaps the trilliums are blooming." She placed the last loaf into a pan.

Soon the trio was strolling leisurely along the back trail. "Here's a trillium, Mother," Ruth said, stopping by a bright white flower that contrasted sharply with its three dark green leaves.

"Oh, good." Mother bent down for a closer look. "They are such a beautiful part of God's creation." She stroked the creamy white petals softly.

Turning to Ruth, she asked, "Can you see anything about the different parts of this flower that is the same?"

Ruth studied it for a few moments. "It has three petals, three sepals, and three leaves. Is that what you meant?"

"Exactly. The word *trillium* comes from the Latin word *tres*, meaning 'three.' It even has more trios than you mentioned. There are six stamens, which are two groups of three. And the stigma, the part of the flower that receives the pollen, is three-lobed at the top."

"I didn't realize that it has so many groups of three." Ruth admired the lovely spring flower. "The Lord has placed so many little details in each thing He has made!"

"Yes, He has." Mother stood up. "Let's see if we can find any other flowers."

Western trillium

David ran down the trail in the lead. "Here's one! Here's one! It's pink!"

Mother and Ruth walked over to him. "Oh, that is another trillium," Mother said.

"But it isn't white." David looked puzzled.
"As the flowers get older, they turn a deep
rose color," Mother explained. "This flower
must have been blooming a while already."

"May I pick it?" Ruth wondered.

"You could," Mother replied. "But you may
want to pick one that just started blooming. It
will last longer."

"All right." Ruth scanned the underbrush
for more trilliums. "There are some over by
that Douglas fir." She pointed toward a nearby
tree. "I think I'll pick one of them."

David started to scamper down the trail.
"Don't go too far ahead, David," Mother called
after him.

"I won't." He stopped abruptly. "Mother,
here's a tr-tr—a flower! May I pick it?"

"Certainly." Mother smiled. "Be sure to pick
it with a long stem so it will fit nicely in our
twelve-inch vase."

"Okay," he cheerfully replied, reaching for
the desired flower.

"Mother, the stinging nettles are coming
up." Ruth rubbed her ankle where she had
brushed against a fine-haired plant.

"We'll have to watch for them then," Mother
said, spotting some more that had sprung up

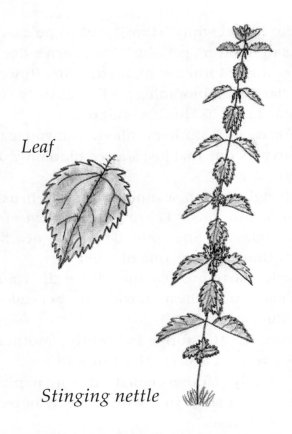

Leaf

Stinging nettle

along the path. "David watch out for the—"

"Ouch! It stung me!" David began to cry. "That fuzzy plant stung me!" Soon tears were streaming down his cheeks.

Mother hurried over to where David was standing. "David, I am sorry. Let me see."

David held up his hand that had small

bumps rising on it. "It hurts," he wailed.

Mother plucked off the fiddlehead of a bracken fern nearby. "This may help." She squeezed as much liquid as she could onto David's hand.

"What's that?" David stopped crying and looked at the fern Mother held.

"It is a bracken fern," Mother answered.

Bracken
fern

"The juice from the young fronds sometimes helps soothe the stinging nettle's sting."

Ruth looked at the hairy green nettle with its heart-shaped leaves. "Why do they sting?"

"The plant contains formic acid," Mother replied. "It is the same acid that is found in insect bites and stings. After the plant is cooked, it doesn't sting anymore."

"Can you eat it?" David wondered.

"Yes," Mother said. "It is an edible plant. But you only want to eat the young plants. And they must be cooked, of course!"

"Or they might sting your mouth," Ruth put in with a grimace.

"That would not be nice!" David exclaimed.

"Mother." Ruth's eyes brightened. "May we have stinging nettles with supper tonight? I want to surprise Joel and Timothy."

Mother smiled down at her. "That would surprise them, all right! I suppose we could, but we'll want to make sure that they are well cooked!"

"But how will we get them into the pan?" Ruth could hardly stand to think of grasping the hairy nettles with her hands.

"I'll use rubber gloves," Mother answered. "After we finish our walk, you can keep Timothy busy while I go and gather the nettles."

"Won't they be surprised?" Ruth laughed.

"I would think so." Mother followed David around a bend in the path.

"Look, Ruth." She paused by a patch of pink flowers scattered among lacy, fernlike leaves. "Here are some bleeding hearts." Mother plucked off one of the flowers near the base of its long stem.

"They are very pretty." Ruth took the lovely flower Mother offered her and added it to her bouquet.

"Why are they heart flowers?" David asked.

"See," Ruth said, holding it out for him to look at. "The flower is shaped like a heart with two pointed petals covering the sides of it."

"Oh, yes."

"Let's add a few more leaves and flowers to your bouquet," Mother suggested, handing Ruth three of the lacy-leafed stalks. "That will make a pleasant centerpiece for our table. We will put the trilliums in our kitchen window."

"Shall I arrange the flowers while you get the nettles?" Ruth asked.

"That would be a good idea." Mother turned to David. "You won't tell the big boys, will you?"

"I won't tell." He shook his head. "I want

Bleeding heart

to see them surprised."

As soon as they got back to the house, Mother slid the bread into the oven. Then she quietly got her gloves and a pan and went in search of some tender young nettles.

"Where's Mother?" Timothy walked into the kitchen.

"She's outside." Ruth looked up from the vase of bleeding-hearts she was arranging. "She should be back in soon."

"I was wondering if supper is almost ready." Timothy rubbed his empty stomach.

"I'm sorry." Ruth grinned. "You know that supper is not for another hour. Father and Joel are not even home yet." Ruth caught a glimpse of Mother coming up the trail.

"But I'm hungry!" Timothy pretended to wail. "That bread smells really good."

"I know what will help get your mind off your stomach." Ruth was thinking fast. "Let's play a game of Take One before I need to help with supper. I'm not very good at it yet, and I need the practice."

"So you want me out of the kitchen?" he guessed correctly. "I know how fond you are of playing Take One! I'm on my way out, especially if there is a surprise in the making."

He went back to the living room and picked up the book he had been reading. "You just keep working. I'll stay in here. And if I may put in an order," Timothy called as he plopped down on the couch, "surprise me with a pie or something!"

Mother caught the end of his statement as she cautiously entered the kitchen. "What?" She gave Ruth a questioning look.

"Timothy guessed that something was going on, and he decided it was in the line of desserts," Ruth whispered. "I hope he's not too disappointed."

"This is better for him than pie." Mother smiled as she took the leaves to the sink to wash them. "These will make a good spinach substitute just this once. But perhaps we should take a cake out of the freezer for dessert. That way he won't be too disappointed."

"I don't smell any pie." Timothy frowned playfully as he sat down at the supper table. "What kept you so busy?"

"Aren't mashed potatoes and fried chicken enough to keep one busy?" Father asked with a smile. Ruth had whispered the secret to him when the boys were not around.

"I suppose," Joel said slowly. "But Timothy

told me they were going to surprise us with something."

After the blessing was asked, Mother lifted the lid on the nettles and put some on David's and her plates.

"What's that funny-smelling stuff?" Timothy wrinkled his nose. "Old, withered spinach?"

David started to open his mouth, but Mother squeezed his leg and gave him a knowing look. He smiled back and shut his lips tightly.

"Now, Timothy," Father rebuked gently. "That is not the way to talk. We will be thankful for what God has given us to eat." He took some "spinach" and handed it to Joel.

"I'm sorry." Timothy watched as Joel took a hearty helping of it and passed it to him.

Joel carefully inspected his "spinach" as he smeared it with butter. Suddenly his eyes lit up with recognition, and he suppressed a smile.

Ruth caught his look and grinned at him as he took his first bite. "Tastes about like spinach," he remarked casually. "Eat it, Timothy. It doesn't taste freezer burnt."

"What is this stuff anyway?" Timothy asked after his first mouthful. "It doesn't taste like old spinach."

"Don't you recognize it?" Ruth started to giggle.

"It's not . . ." Timothy bent over his "spinach." "It is . . . it's not . . . it's not stinging nettles, is it?" he asked suddenly.

"How did you guess?" Joel playfully patted him on the back. "It doesn't taste too bad."

"No," Timothy admitted. "But I just knew spinach didn't have hairs!"

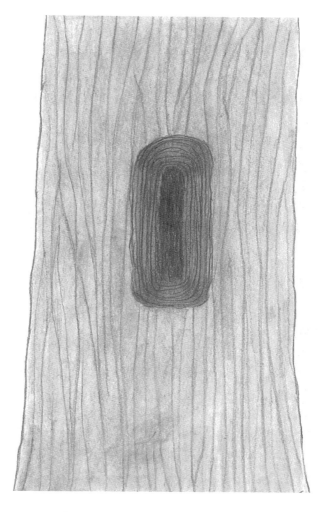

CHAPTER NINE

"The trees of the Lord are full of sap; the cedars of Lebanon, which he hath planted; where the birds make their nests."

Psalm 104:16, 17

The Cedar's Friend

Ruth caught sight of a dark crowlike shadow scooting along the ground.

Kuk! Kuk!

She quickly brought her gaze upward. "What?" she gasped. "What type of bird is that?"

The black-and-white figure swept through the trees, flapping its wings at irregular intervals, and landed on a nearby Douglas fir.

"Let's see," Ruth observed. "White, black,

and red-crested head; black back; and white on its wings. I'll have to look it up. It's a woodpecker, but it's a big woodpecker. It must be over a foot long!"

Suddenly the large bird left his perch on the side of the Douglas fir and vanished into the forest.

"I'm going to look him up right now," Ruth decided as she hurried to the house.

"Here it is, Mother." She walked into the kitchen a few minutes later, bird book in hand. "This is the bird I told you about."

"Oh, a pileated woodpecker!" Mother exclaimed, looking over Ruth's shoulder. "What a special blessing to see one of those."

"Yes," Ruth agreed. "This book says they are uncommon and wary. I'm thankful that the Lord gave me the privilege of seeing one."

A few days later, Timothy was standing outside the goat pen. "Almost full." He glanced down at the water bucket he was filling with a hose on the other side of the fence. "You were thirsty yesterday, Biscuit Doe," he said to the white nanny who was watching him.

Kuk! Kuk! Kuk! Kuk!

Timothy heard a flapping of wings overhead. A pair of pileated woodpeckers landed

Pileated woodpecker

on a cedar tree twenty-five feet away.

"Look at those birds," he whispered. "I haven't seen anything like them before."

One of the birds began drumming on the side of the tree, while the other perched above him. *Tap! Tap! Tap! Tap!*

"I wonder if they are making a nest," Timothy thought. "I should go get Ruth." He carefully made his way out of sight and went back to the house.

"Ruth, come quickly!" He burst into the house. "There are some interesting birds out here! They might be making a nest. They are some type of woodpecker."

Timothy and Ruth softly crept near the cedar tree. "It looks as if they're taking turns." Ruth watched them intently. "Look at the big chips of wood they are pecking out of the tree. I hope they won't kill it. That is such a pretty tree."

"So do I," Timothy agreed. "It's one of my favorite trees."

Before long, the woodpeckers flew away. "It would be nice if they made their nest here." Ruth walked over to the cedar tree. "See how big this hole is already!"

"Yes." Timothy studied the large, rectangular depression. "And look at this huge chip of wood." He bent over and picked up a whitish chunk of cedar wood. "It must be an inch wide and an inch and a half long. They must really peck hard!"

"Except for the rare ivory-billed wood-pecker, they are the largest woodpecker in North America," Ruth told him. "They surely can make big holes fast. I was reading that they prefer old growth or second growth forests. It said they will come near houses in those forests. That must be why we have them so close here."

"What do they eat?" Timothy asked.

"I'm not sure," Ruth replied. "Probably insects—let's go look it up."

"In this book," Ruth began a few minutes later, "it says they eat tree-destroying insects, such as carpenter ants. They do little damage to the tree, considering all the destructive insects they eat."

"That's good to know." Timothy looked up from the bird book he had. "I remember see-ing sawdust piles from carpenter ants at the base of that tree. Maybe that was what they were after."

"Probably," Ruth agreed.

"I was reading about their nests," he went

on. "And it says they are usually anywhere from twelve to eighty feet off the ground. They build a new nest every year. The nest cavities are usually three feet deep, and it takes them almost a month to make them."

"That is a long time," Ruth said. "I don't think they are making a nest there, but at least they are helping our cedar tree."

"Yes," Timothy agreed. "That's good. Let's show Father the hole as soon as he gets home from work. Then maybe he'll give us a lesson on cedar trees!"

It was after supper when Father and the children headed for the cedar tree. *Tap, tap, tap* greeted their ears as they neared it.

"They must be back," Ruth whispered as they came in full view of the tree.

"Yes, I can see them," Father said softly. "They are very interesting-looking birds."

The woodpeckers took turns pecking for a while and then flew deeper into the forest.

"The things God has created are many and varied." Father spoke first. "His wisdom is far, far above ours? He even planned for woodpeckers to help protect the trees from destructive insects. All of creation is in a delicate balance, planned by God Himself, from the tiniest insect to the tallest tree."

"Speaking of trees . . ." Timothy began.

Father laughed. "I suppose that you'd like another tree lesson?"

"Yes, please." Ruth smiled. "May we learn about the cedar tree today?"

"The cedar we have here is called the western red cedar," Father told them. "It is a member of the cypress, or cedar, family." He reached up and plucked a twig. "The cedar doesn't shed its lower branches as easily as the Douglas fir does, so it is easier for me to reach a fresh branch."

M-ma-a-a. Biscuit Doe looked longingly at the treat Father held in his hand.

"Oh." Father chuckled. "Someone else would like a closer look at a cedar branch too. Be patient, Biscuit, you may have this when we're finished."

He held the fragrant, dark yellow green branch out to Timothy and Ruth. "Its sprigs are like ferns with flat, scaly leaves."

"The edges are rather rough." Ruth ran her fingers along a thin, narrow leaf.

"Yes," Father agreed as he crushed a piece in his fingers. "Doesn't that have a rich, evergreen smell?" He held it out to them, but before

112

Western red cedar

they could sniff it, Biscuit Doe seized the opportunity and snatched the branch over the fence.

"Oh, Biscuit." Ruth laughed. "Where is your
patience?"

"Now that our specimen has been
snatched," Father said with a chuckle, "it must

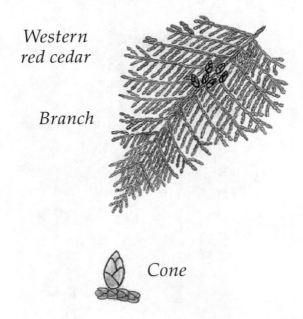

*Western
red cedar*

Branch

Cone

be time to study the bark." He walked over to
the trunk and pulled off a string of cinnamon
gray bark. "What do you notice?"

"It has loose, stringy bark," Ruth replied.

"That's right," Father agreed. "The Indians

wove the bark into clothing. And because the wood is buoyant and water resistant, they used it for their canoes. Today it is widely used for roofing shingles because of its weather resistant properties."

"How tall do cedar trees grow?" Timothy wondered.

"The average western red cedar is 150 to 200 feet tall and 4 to 8 feet in diameter," Father answered. "The tallest can grow up to 250 feet."

Ruth picked up a small red brown cone. "Is this a cedar cone?" She held it for Father to see.

"Yes, it is," he replied. "The cones drop their seeds in late August, but the cones themselves don't drop off until the following spring. Little cones only one-third to one-half inch long don't seem to fit such a large tree, do they?"

"Not really." Timothy studied the little brown cone. "It is a tiny cone."

"Maybe tomorrow I can tell you about another big tree with small cones," Father said. "See if you can find it by then."

CHAPTER TEN

"For ye shall go out with joy, and be led forth with peace: the mountains and the hills shall break forth before you into singing, and all the trees of the field shall clap their hands."

Isaiah 55:12

Drooping Peaks

"I think we found your tree, Father," Timothy announced at the supper table the following day. "It has long, drooping branches and a bent-over crown."

"It sounds as if you found the right tree," Father affirmed. "After the dishes are washed, let's all take a walk up to what you call Sunset Point. There are quite a few hemlocks on the way there."

Dishes were done in record time, and even Timothy lent a hand. "I haven't seen you dry dishes so fast in a long time," Ruth teased, placing a cup on the drainer.

Timothy pretended ignorance as he swished his towel rapidly over a plate. "Are we almost finished?"

"Yes." Mother smiled at his eagerness.

"You mentioned the bent peak or top of the western hemlock, Timothy," Father began as they stepped outside. "That 'drooping peak' is one normal characteristic to look for. It makes it easier to tell the western hemlock and the Douglas fir apart."

"Often Douglas fir, western red cedar, and western hemlock grow together, don't they?" Joel wondered.

"Yes," Father replied. "The latter two especially prefer a lot of rainfall." He led the way down a narrow path lined with thick underbrush, and started down into a small gully.

Stopping by a large hemlock, he laid his hand on the russet brown bark. "Take note of the shallow vertical grooves that make small, uneven plates all along the trunk. Here's a horizontal crack too." He pointed to a crack running around the tree. "Douglas firs don't have them." He began the descent again.

Once in the gully, Father stopped by a young hemlock. "Let's study the needles. The flat green needles run in two rows on the sides of the twig. There is a third row of shorter needles

*Hemlock branch
and cones*

on the top too. Can you see them?"

Ruth came over. "Yes, I can."

Father flipped up the branch so that they could see the underside. "Each needle has two white stripes on the bottom. This makes the

Western hemlock

underside look silver green compared to the dark, shiny upperside.

"Western hemlock is another important lumber tree." Father started up the hill on the other side of the gully. "Its light yellow wood has a straight grain." He held a branch back so that the rest could pass by.

"How tall do western hemlock trees grow?" Timothy asked, stepping gingerly over a mountain beaver hole.

"Most of them are 125 to 175 feet tall and two to four feet in diameter," Father replied. "They are one of the biggest trees in Washington." He mounted the top of the hill.

"Do you want to take the lead now?" he asked Joel. "You children know the best way to get to the vantage point of the big stump."

"Sure." Joel stepped off into the underbrush to pass Father. "You just go under this fallen tree and climb up on the big rotting log and— what happened here?" He stopped abruptly.

Timothy almost collided into him. "Why, there's a hole in this log!"

"You know, boys," Father said inspecting the hole, "I believe this is the work of a bear."

"A bear?" Timothy's eyes rounded. "Why would he have done that?"

"He must have been hunting for some insects, possibly ants," Father answered. "I found some signs of a bear on the back trail not too long ago."

Ruth climbed onto the log and peered into

the hole. "You should see it from here, David."

"I want to." He scrambled up with Father's help. "Bears are big, aren't they, Father?" he asked with wide eyes as he saw the large hole. "Why did that bear have to make a big hole in our log? Will I see that bear?"

"To answer your first question," Father began with a smile, "yes, bears are quite big— at least some of them are. This was probably the work of a black bear though. They are the smallest of our bears."

"If they are small bears, are they still bigger than I am?" David wondered.

Mother put an arm around David. "Black bears are 4½ to 6½ feet long. That would be a bear as long as Ruth is tall to one all the way up to a little bit longer than Father is tall."

"Oh." David looked from Ruth to Father and from Father to Ruth. "They are still big."

Father scratched his head. "I remember reading that black bears eat mainly vegetation. But they also will eat small mammals, fish, eggs, honey, garbage, and ants' eggs. I think he made that hole to get some ant eggs."

"But how did he know the ants were there?" Ruth wondered. "I thought bears cannot see very well."

"God gave bears good ears and noses," Joel answered her. "Our bear probably either heard or smelled the ants."

"To change the subject," Mother interjected, "I think we should get to our vantage point.

Black bear

The sun is starting to set."

"That's right!" Timothy scrambled up onto the log after Joel. "I almost forgot what we came up here for."

The clouds were lit with pink and gold as the bright orb sank into the west while they stood watching. "'Beyond the sunset . . . '" Mother began to sing softly, and the rest joined her worshipfully.

The silvery chirping of a robin rang clearly through the evening air. Near the horizon, the gray clouds were streaked with crimson while the cirrus clouds above them took on a rich purple hue.

"'The heavens declare the glory of God; and the firmament sheweth his handywork,'" Father quoted. "'Day unto day uttereth speech and night unto night sheweth knowledge.' God's infinite wisdom and power are displayed in creation about us for all to see and hear. Great is our God!"

"'And greatly to be praised,'" Mother added.

"But now it is growing dark, Father." Mother helped David off his stumpy perch.

"Yes, we should be going." Father turned for one last look at the silver-tinted clouds and started down the gully.

CHAPTER ELEVEN

"The flowers appear on the earth; the time of the singing of birds is come."
Song of Solomon 2:12

God's Tiny Jewels

Buzz. Buzz.

With a start, Timothy looked up from the flower bed he was weeding as a surprise for Mother that afternoon.

Buzz. Buzz.

He spotted a tiny rufous form on the budding raspberry stalks next to him.

"A hummingbird," he whispered, admiring the wee creature that had paused for a rest.

Buzz-z-z. The little bird darted off.

Timothy jumped to his feet. "I'm going to tell Ruth! She'll want to hang the humming-bird feeder out right away."

"Guess what!" He burst into the house.

"You must have made a mud pie," Ruth teased, eyeing his filthy hands.

"No." Timothy grinned. "This is a lot better than a mud pie."

"I wouldn't know." Ruth studied her brother's face.

"I saw a hummingbird."

"Really?" Ruth exclaimed more than asked. She glanced over at the calendar. "It is the end of March. They are on time. I almost forgot they were coming. I'd better hang up the feeder as soon as I can."

"May I make some hummingbird syrup, Mother?" Ruth asked as she came upstairs with the feeder.

"Certainly." Mother smiled. "Remember, it is one part sugar to four parts water. Put four cups of water in a pan and bring it to a boil. After it boils, add one cup of sugar and stir until it is dissolved. When it is cooled you may put some in the feeder."

"All right." Ruth stooped, reached into the

open cupboard and took out a pan.

"Why don't we use honey to sweeten it?" she asked while she was waiting for the water to boil. "It seems as though that would be better for them."

"I know," Mother agreed. "But honey is too strong for them and can make them very sick. That is why we don't want to use it."

As soon as the syrup was cool, Ruth filled the feeder.

"There," she said as she hung it in front of the kitchen window. "I wonder how long it will be before they start coming."

"Look what's in the kitchen window." Father smiled as he walked into the room that evening. "Have any hummingbirds come yet?"

"Not that I know of," Ruth replied. "I do hope they start coming soon."

"Look!" Timothy exclaimed, pointing to the window. "There's one now! Maybe he remembered it from last year."

"O-o-oh, he's pretty." David stared at the little red brown bird with green on his head and wings.

Suddenly the little bird turned, and the light struck his chin feathers just right.

"He's shiny red!" David exclaimed. "I

thought that was a black spot."

The sudden outburst startled the bird, and he quickly buzzed away.

"Why is he so red?" David wondered.

"God gave him special feathers," Father explained. "And when the light shines on them from a certain direction, it makes them look bright, shiny red."

"There he is," Joel pointed out. "See? He is on that cedar branch. You can see his red chin patch clearly."

"Yes, I can see him." Timothy peered out the window.

Ruth had gone in search of her bird book and came back flipping its pages rapidly. "Here he is—a male rufous hummingbird. It looks as though we could have black-chinned and Anna's hummingbirds visiting here as well."

"It does." Joel looked over her shoulder at the maps. "But we haven't seen either kind in all the years we've had a feeder. Maybe they don't come into our exact area."

"Are there many different hummingbirds?" David wondered.

"Yes," Mother answered. "Here in the Western Hemisphere, we have about 343 kinds. Hummingbirds are the second largest family

Rufous hummingbirds
Male at feeder
Female below

of birds that we have."

"O-o-oh." David looked out the window at the feeder again.

"Did you know that hummingbirds can beat their wings seventy-five times a second when flying?" Joel asked Ruth.

"No," Ruth answered. "How many times a minute would that be?"

Joel stopped to figure briefly. "Four thousand five hundred!"

"How can they do it?" Timothy's question was an exclamation.

"They can fly forward, backward, up, down, and even sideways," Father put in. "Their wings are set in ball-and-socket joints, making it possible for them to rotate their wings in complete circles."

"How did he stop by the feeder?" David wondered. "He just stood still in midair."

"That is called hovering," Mother replied. "They hover by moving their wings forward and backward in a figure eight so they don't move anywhere. Their wings only go fifty to fifty-five beats a second while they are hovering."

"That would be three thousand beats a minute." Joel had been doing some quick mental calculating. "Amazingly fast."

"All of God's creation is truly amazing," Father commented. "From the tiniest hummingbird to the largest ostrich."

The next afternoon Ruth posed by the feeder, holding her fingers up as perches under the feeding holes.

"Sore arms?" Timothy asked, pausing with an armload of firewood to watch her.

Ruth nodded. "A male rufous almost sat on my finger. He was so pretty."

Buzz-z-z-z-z-z! A tiny hummer zipped by Timothy's head and zoomed up to the feeder. *Buzz! Buzz!* He got closer and closer to Ruth's fingers.

Quickly he took a sip of sugar water. Ruth held her breath. He came back for a longer drink. Slowly she edged her finger under him. Gently, he perched on her finger and studied her with his little beady black eyes. He pertly tucked his wings to his sides and took another sip. Then, *Buzz-z-z.* As suddenly as he had come, he was gone.

"Was it Mr. Buzz, Ruth?" Timothy asked, thinking of the bold male rufous who had been their annual visitor for the last few years.

"I think so," Ruth replied. "He acted as

though he had perched on fingers before."

"Mr. Buzz sat on my finger today," Ruth announced at the supper table.

"Could you feel him?" David wondered.

"Hardly," Ruth answered with a giggle. "I read somewhere that hummingbirds weigh no more than a penny."

"That isn't very heavy." David put a spoonful of soup into his mouth.

"Up to 30 percent of their weight is flight muscles," Mother told them. "God made them to be compact little flying machines."

"Their feet are so little," Ruth remarked. "I enjoy looking at them when the birds are perched on my fingers."

"They are also weak," Father added. "Hummingbirds can never walk but will make small hops only on rare occasions. Most of the time they use their wings, even to move down a branch."

"What do they eat when people don't feed them?" David asked.

"They eat nectar from flowers and also spiders and gnats," Mother said as she put another ladleful of soup into Joel's outstretched bowl. "They catch gnats in midair, and they take insects out of spider webs. Sometimes they even take the spiders themselves!"

"How do they get the nectar out of flowers?" David questioned.

"God gave them long, strawlike tongues," Mother answered, "that are shaped like a *w* at the bottom. They suck up nectar through their tongues."

"To have enough energy to fly, they must feed every ten to fifteen minutes," Father told them. "In one day, they can eat five times their body weight in food, and drink eight times their body weight in water."

"There's a female." Timothy pointed to a tiny bird with a shiny green back and a rust-and-white breast that was hovering at the feeder.

"They have such long beaks!" David watched her poke her beak into the feeder.

"Yes. That is for reaching deep into flowers that bees and butterflies cannot get into," Father explained. "Their tongues are even longer. God made hummingbirds for pollinating flowers that His other creatures could not."

The female darted away as another tiny bird approached the feeder.

"They fly so fast," Ruth commented.

"It looks that way," Joel agreed. "But they

usually don't fly faster than any other bird. They are so small that they appear to be going faster than they really are."

"That's right." Father reached for another biscuit. "However, some hummingbirds, like the Anna's hummingbird, can go up to sixty miles per hour in their dives. They use their tails to help stop them at the bottom of their dives."

"Hummingbirds surely are interesting creatures," Ruth remarked.

"Marvelous are His works," Father agreed.

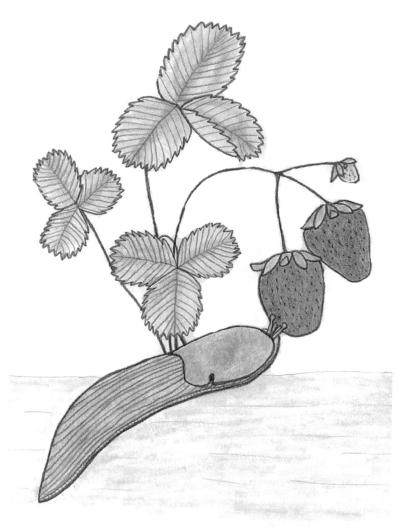

CHAPTER TWELVE

Slimy and Long

"It's time to plant the garden," Father decided one Saturday in early April. "I don't think we'll be having any more frosts."

"All right." Mother flipped another pancake. "Will you be turning the soil after breakfast?"

"Yes," he replied with a nod. "I'll rototill a patch for the corn and the potatoes while Joel and Timothy turn the soil in the raised beds. We'll let you know when we are ready to plant."

"That will suit me fine." Mother put another stack of pancakes into the oven to keep warm. "Perhaps Ruth and I will weed the strawberries while you are doing that. I noticed the other day that the weeds are starting to take over."

The shrill ringing of the telephone interrupted the usual breakfast chatter. Father hurried to answer it.

"Hello, Millers . . . Really? . . . Praise the Lord. . . . No, I'm sure it will suit. I'll talk to Ellen and let you know. This is a real answer to prayer! Good-bye."

All eyes looked expectantly at Father as he returned to his seat at the table. "It must be good news, Father." Mother smiled. "You look very glad."

"I am." Father nodded. "Grandfather just heard from Uncle Elmer, and he says we can come visit him. Grandfather would like to go early next week and take us along. Will that suit you, Mother?"

"Surely." Mother's eyes glowed. "That is a real answer to prayer."

After a refreshing time of family worship, they all headed for the garden, merrily discussing the plans for their trip to the coast.

"This surely needed to be done," Ruth

remarked, tugging on a dandelion in the strawberry bed. "Weeds grow so quickly!"

"They certainly do," Mother agreed. "It's good we are taking care of this before we

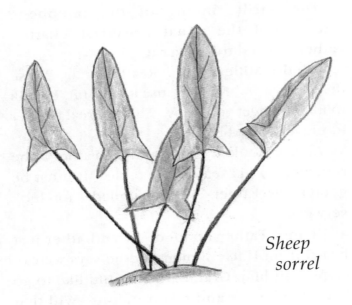

Sheep sorrel

leave." She was uprooting a patch of sheep sorrel. "Please try to get all the roots if you come across some sheep sorrel," Mother told her. "They usually lead to another plant nearby and to another near that and to another and so on. We don't want to let them spread. See all the

tiny sorrel plants starting to grow on this root?"
Mother held up a long piece of sorrel root for
her to see.

"Yes." Ruth grabbed another dandelion and
pulled. "O-o-oh!" She quickly drew her hand
back. "That's a terrible feeling!"

"Did you get poked by a sticker bush?" Joel
asked from his vantage point on the edge of a
raised bed.

"No, it was worse than that," she replied.

Joel turned another shovelful of dirt. "I
think I know." He smiled. "Was it long and
slimy?"

"Yes!" Ruth said emphatically, with a
grimace. "You guessed it!"

"Oh, what's wrong with a little slug?" Timothy dug his shovel into the ground and came
over to inspect his sister's find.

"But—" he paused, stooping over the dandelion with the slug and pulling it out of the
ground— "they certainly are slimy." He shook
his hand after dropping the weed into the
bucket as if trying to shake off the slime. "I see
what you mean." He rubbed his hand with
some dirt to try to remove it. "I haven't picked
up a slug for a while."

"Well, Timothy." Mother smiled up at him

as she pulled another weed. "I suppose you deserved that for teasing your sister so. Why don't you go and attempt to wash it off? There's no reason to get the shovel handle all slimy."

"Sorry, sis," Timothy apologized. "I'll try to put my hand where you did before I tease you next time."

"Where did that slug go?" David left his sandbox and came running. "I want to see it. May I take it to Uncle Elmer?"

"Oh, no, your hands will get all slimy." Mother suppressed a smile. "You don't want to pick one up, and I'm sure Uncle Elmer has plenty of slugs where he lives."

"May I see it?" he pleaded.

"He's buried in my bucket now," Ruth told him. "But maybe we'll find another one." She grimaced at the thought.

Suddenly she asked, "What is a slug, anyway? A snail?"

"That's correct," Mother replied. "A slug is related to the snail. They belong to the mollusk family, along with clams and octopuses."

"Really?" Ruth finished the row she had been working on and moved to another. "I didn't know that."

"Yes, it's true." Mother pulled up some

chickweed. "Mollusks are the largest group of animals that God has made. Only the insect group has more species."

"Slugs don't look much like snails though," Ruth remarked. "How can they be snails?"

"They are snails without outer shells," Joel said. "I studied them once. Did you know that God gave them two sets of tentacles? The pair closest to the front of the slug is for feeling, and the other pair farther back has their eyes on the ends of them."

"Here's a slug!" David announced cheerily. "Shall I bring him to you?"

"You had better not," Mother told him. "You will get your hands very slimy. I will come and see it." She stood to her feet and walked over to him.

"Ruth, come here, please." Mother bent over for a closer look. "I want to show you something."

Ruth dropped her trowel and came. "What?" she wondered.

"See that little hole on the right side of his back?" Mother pointed. "That is where he takes in air. Under his mantle, the fleshy covering that protects his organs, he has a lunglike cavity. This hole is where the air goes in."

"What do slugs eat?" David wondered.

"Well," Joel answered, "they eat our lettuce and cabbage and strawberries and flowers and whatever else suits their taste."

"That's not nice of them." David frowned. "I do not like slug bites in my strawberries!"

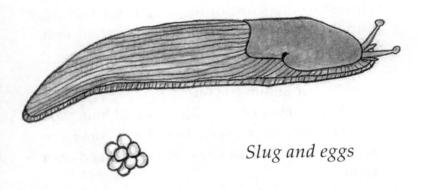

Slug and eggs

"But God gave slugs a job to do too," Mother told him. "They eat decaying leaves to break them down. That helps to keep the ground from getting deeply covered with leaves."

"But why do we have so-o-o many slugs?" Ruth asked.

"They like wet, shaded areas," Joel replied.

"And our area is certainly damp and shady. Maybe keeping the strawberry patch free of weeds will give them less shade to hide in," he said with a grin.

"How do they move?" Timothy had returned with somewhat improved hands.

"They have a foot, a large muscle that they use for moving slowly across the ground," Mother answered him.

"Why do they leave a slimy trail?" Ruth pulled another dandelion after closely inspecting it.

"The slime lubricates the foot to help them move," Mother replied.

"Mother, what are these white, almost clear things on this dandelion root?" Ruth held it up for her to see.

Mother smiled. "They came from your slimy friend."

Ruth quickly dropped the dandelion. "Oh, slug eggs!"

"They lay their eggs in the soil," Joel informed her.

"I guess I just can't escape them," Ruth groaned.

"Western Washington is slug country," Timothy said seriously with a twinkle in his

Timothy slipping on slug

eyes as he moved from one raised garden bed to the next. "You will just have to accept the fact—whoa!" He slipped and caught his fall with his hands. Startled, he looked around for the cause of his fall. Suddenly he burst out laughing. "As I was saying," he continued, "we all need to accept the indisputable fact that . . . that . . . you could slip on a banana slug anytime!"

CHAPTER THIRTEEN

"He watereth the hills from his chambers: the earth is satisfied with the fruit of thy works."

Psalm 104:13

To Uncle Elmer's

"Will we get to Uncle Elmer's soon?" David wondered, stretching his arms and yawning broadly.

"Yes, we will be there soon," Father answered patiently.

Grandfather Miller bent over the map and then glanced over the directions Uncle Elmer had given him. "Turn right at the next crossroads, and follow it for about five miles until it comes to a T. Turn left at the T. His lane is the second one to the right." He paused. "He said it is a very long lane. He has no really close neighbors."

After winding back and forth through groves of massive trees, they came upon a tiny, moss-covered cabin. Sunlight filtered through a break in the clouds and lit up the green hue of the cabin. "This must be it," Father decided.

At the sound of the approaching car, a tall, wiry man appeared in the driveway. As soon as the car stopped, Uncle Elmer rushed over to meet Grandfather with tears in his eyes. "It has been so long, John. And, Mark, how your family has grown! Oh, I wish I would have said you could come sooner."

The boisterous supply of energy David displayed in getting out of the car vanished as Uncle Elmer came over to shake his hand. He clung tightly to Mother's skirt and whispered, "Hello."

"Hello, young man." Uncle Elmer gave him a hearty handshake and a broad smile.

The huge stand of trees seemed to dwarf the small cabin even more, and the light in the clearing grew dimmer as a gray sky chased away the break in the clouds. "Is it going to rain?" Timothy wondered.

"Will it rain?" Uncle Elmer chuckled. "My boy, I live near the Olympic rain forest, one of the wettest places in the United States. We average twelve feet of rain a year here."

"Twelve feet!" Timothy whistled. "And I thought *we* get a lot of rain. Why ever do you get so much?" Timothy felt a drop splash on his nose.

"The Olympic Mountains reach almost to the sea at this point. The warm, moist air from the Pacific is forced over these mountains and drops much moisture as it rises and cools. The cooler the air is, the less moisture it can hold," Uncle Elmer explained.

"This is one of the three places in the world where there is a temperate rain forest. The temperatures are mild. They usually stay between 32 and 80 degrees Fahrenheit. That is why my forest is moist, mossy, and dense."

The drops started to fall faster. "We'd better get out of the rain." So saying, Uncle Elmer led the way into his tiny cabin.

Once they were crowded into his two-room abode, he said, "I hope you don't mind, men, but I thought we'd let the womenfolk have the bedroom. I borrowed a big tent from one of my friends for us to use as sleeping quarters."

"That will be fine," Grandfather assured him. "I don't think my bones are too old for that; at least I hope they aren't."

Uncle Elmer chuckled. "I found cots for us older gentlemen, John."

Joel noticed that Uncle Elmer was trying very hard to be cheerful but that whenever he stopped laughing, a sad look came into his eyes. Joel breathed a silent prayer for him.

Uncle Elmer was eager to show them all the treasures of the forest, so he proposed a walk as soon as the rain stopped.

"Here, Ruth," he said, handing her a small field guide. "See how many ferns you can find. They like the rain forest."

Soon Uncle Elmer was guiding them up a narrow, winding trail. "It is very moist and mossy," Ruth remarked, noticing the thick moss on the tree trunks.

"It just rained," Timothy teased. "But you are right. Almost everything but the pathway is green—oh, here's a fern for you, Ruth." He grasped a long, stiff frond. "Can you find this one?" he asked with a twinkle.

"Can I *find* it?" Ruth laughed. "We have lots of sword ferns at home, Timothy Miller!"

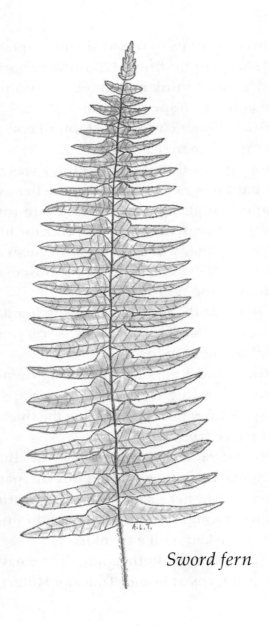

Sword fern

"There are some ferns in this tree, Ruth," Joel pointed out.

Ruth glanced quickly over several pages. "Are they licorice ferns, Uncle Elmer?"

"That's right," he affirmed. "See their small, leathery fronds. But can you guess why they

Licorice fern

are called *licorice* ferns?"

Ruth shook her head and then looked at the description in the book. "Oh, it is because their roots taste somewhat like licorice."

Uncle Elmer nodded. "And here is a maidenhair fern," he pointed out. "See how the

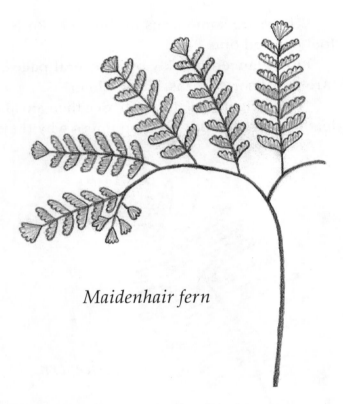

Maidenhair fern

delicate fan-shaped leaves cling to the brown, wiry stems. The stems bend in a horseshoe shape."

"That is a very pretty fern." Ruth stepped over to get a closer look. "I like that one best of all."

The dense canopy over their heads lightened somewhat as they approached another clearing. "This is one of my favorite spots." Uncle Elmer motioned toward the clearing.

A small, shimmering lake stood sunken in the immense forest. "Tomorrow morning I'd like to bring anyone who is interested up here," he told them. "Often elk come to this clearing in the early morning hours."

"I would like to come," Timothy spoke up first.

"Can you be an early riser?" Uncle Elmer asked in a teasing tone.

Father smiled. "I think most of us would be very willing to get up early to see such a treat," he told Uncle Elmer. "The Lord has made so many lovely creatures for us to enjoy."

Just then David walked over to Uncle Elmer and took Uncle Elmer's worn hand into his small, chubby one. His earnest blue eyes looked right into Uncle Elmer's. "Do you know God?" he asked suddenly.

Uncle Elmer's eyes looked very sad. "I used to, my boy," he whispered.

"Well, I wish you still did," David declared in his childlike manner. "I like you very much."

David did not notice the tears that gathered in Uncle Elmer's eyes. "Shall we go back and get supper now?" he asked quietly.

Grandfather and Father looked at each other with hope shining in their eyes. Uncle Elmer did seem close to the kingdom.

The next morning a group of sleepy-eyed travelers trudged up the path after Uncle Elmer. The snowcapped Olympic Mountains glowed pink with the sunrise.

"Now quiet, everyone," Uncle Elmer cautioned as they neared the lake. "One noise and we may not see anything. At least we are downwind of the lake this morning, so the elk will not be able to detect our scent.

"Sh-h-h-h." He came to a halt and pointed.

Two large elk stood in a small clump of deciduous trees along the edge of the water.

"They're beautiful," Mother said softly.

David tugged on Uncle Elmer's pant leg. "May I go pet them?"

"Oh, no, David," Uncle Elmer whispered. "They are wild and unsafe to pet."

"But I want to feel their fuzzy fur." David stared at the huge creatures.

Uncle Elmer shook his head, smiling. "You don't really want to, David. I think those are both bull elk. They are large enough. This time of year they don't have antlers."

When the elk disappeared into the dense

Roosevelt elk (bulls) in late summer

forest, everyone sat down beside the lake to enjoy a picnic breakfast.

"Aren't female elk called cows?" Ruth wondered as she poured milk over her granola.

"That's correct." Uncle Elmer nodded. "Elk are usually found in herds with several cows and two or three bulls."

"Where are the cows then?" Timothy wondered. "There were none with those bulls."

"These must be stags or full-grown bulls," Uncle Elmer replied. "They stay in groups by themselves, and then when they are able, they will fight with a herd bull to have a herd of their own. The elk around here are Roosevelt elk, which are larger than their cousins in the Rocky Mountains. They also have lighter rump patches than those farther east."

"I didn't realize that," Father replied. "Remember when we stopped at Yellowstone National Park years ago, Grandfather?"

"How could I forget?" Grandfather chuckled. "That black, moonlit night when I took you down the hill by the campground to look for animals in the meadow . . . "

"And I was wondering if we would see any animals on the way," Father put in.

"And suddenly . . . " Grandfather started

laughing too hard to finish right away.

"And suddenly what?" The children sat in rapt attention.

"Suddenly," he continued, catching his breath, "we heard a loud bugle! It sounded as though a bull elk was right behind us!"

"I spun around quite fast, didn't I?" Father chuckled at the memory. "I thought he would surely get us before we ever got back up that hill! But he was really bugling down in the meadow, some distance from us."

"I would have spun around too." Ruth remembered the eight-hundred-pound creatures they had just seen.

"Would you mind if we had family worship here this morning, Elmer?" Grandfather asked.

"Just go ahead," Uncle Elmer consented.

Grandfather took a small New Testament out of his pocket and read a chapter of the precious Word. Melodious singing soon rang through the dense forest. Uncle Elmer sat with his head bowed and listened.

CHAPTER FOURTEEN

"Let the field be joyful, and all that is therein: then shall all the trees of the wood rejoice before the Lord: for he cometh."

Psalm 96:12, 13

Red Wood

"Father." Ruth walked over to where he was sanding a bookcase. "There are some pretty reddish purple flowers in the woods. When you have time, would you please come and tell me what they are?"

"I can come now." Father put down the piece of sandpaper he was using. "Why don't you get Timothy too. We can have another tree lesson while we're at it."

"All right," Ruth said, running to find him.

A few minutes later she was leading the way down the back trail. "There are the flowers, Father." She pointed to several flowers on the twigs of a six-foot bush that was just beginning to leaf out.

"Oh, yes." Father recognized them. "Those are salmonberry flowers."

"May I pick them for Mother?" Timothy asked, starting into the undergrowth.

"Certainly," Father replied. "There should be more flowers on the bush soon. But watch out—" It was too late.

"Ouch!" Timothy dropped his grip on the dry, thorny branch he had grasped to keep his balance. "They have thorns!"

"I was just about to warn you." Father came to help him. "The older shoots have sharp thorns. The younger branches don't have such large, sharp ones," he said, reaching up and carefully plucking off a twig. "See." He held the flowers out to Timothy.

"Yes." Timothy nodded. "Thank you for getting them for me. Shall I quickly take them in to Mother?"

"That would be a good idea." Father made his way back to the trail. "We'll have another

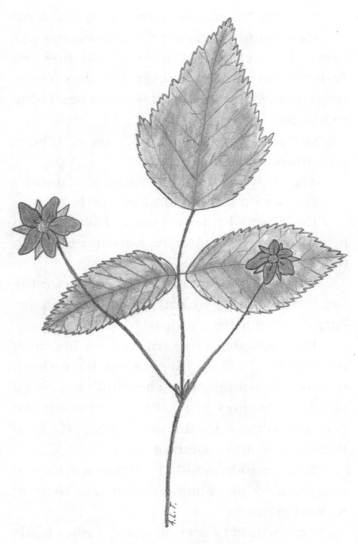

Salmonberry flowers

tree lesson when you get back."

Soon they were making their way along the trail again. "Our tree for today is deciduous, which means that it loses its leaves each year. Who can guess what it is?"

"An alder?" Ruth pointed to a trunk two feet in diameter that they had stopped by.

"That's correct," Father answered. "A red alder is exactly what I had in mind."

Timothy looked at the light gray bark with small, raised bumps. "The bark is certainly smooth compared to the western hemlock and the Douglas fir. And yet red alders are tall trees too." He looked into the leafy canopy above his head.

"They are a tall tree," Father agreed. "They grow anywhere from 80 to 130 feet tall on the average. And they can grow quickly. It is possible for them to be 35 to 40 feet tall when they are only ten years old!"

"Oh!" Ruth exclaimed, looking at a smaller alder beside her. "No wonder this little tree seems to be getting big so fast! I've noticed that it is quite a bit taller than it was last year."

"See how big its leaves are?" Father asked as he plucked off a leaf five inches long and three inches wide. "The teeth on the leaves are

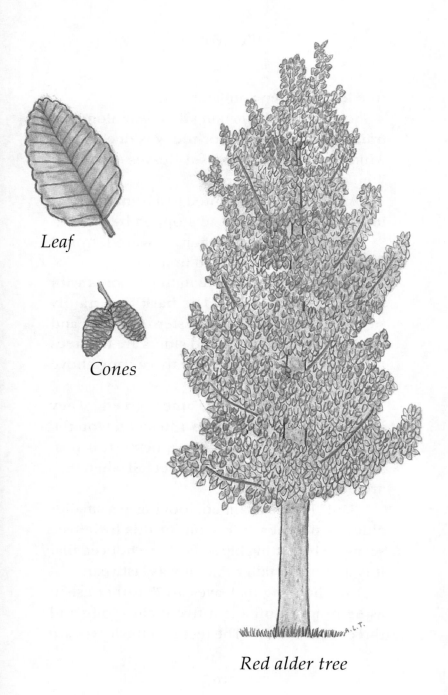

Leaf

Cones

Red alder tree

uneven and rough-looking."

"They are lighter on the underside, aren't they?" Ruth turned over a smooth, dark green leaf. "They look almost white underneath."

"Is this an alder cone?" Timothy asked, picking up a three-quarter-inch, oval-shaped cone.

"Yes," Father answered, picking up one lying by his feet. "See how thick the scales are for such a little cone? They feel rather woody compared to the other cones we've studied."

"Do people use red alder wood for anything?" Timothy wondered.

"Yes," Father replied. "In fact, it is Washington's most important hardwood. They use its wood for furniture, firewood, and smoking meats."

"A hardwood is a deciduous tree, right?" Ruth wanted to know.

Father picked up another cone. "That's right. Softwoods are the evergreen conifer trees like cedar and fir."

"But why is it called *red* alder?" Timothy questioned with a puzzled frown. "The only thing red that I see are these few rust-colored hairs on the bottom of this leaf."

Father chuckled. "I remember asking Uncle Elmer that same question when I was your age.

He told me that shortly after the wood is cut, it turns a bright red. When you first cut it, it looks creamy white, but soon it turns red. Sap from an alder tree contains tannic acid, which turns red when it dries.

"Red alder is a member of the birch family and is our most common broadleaf tree," he went on. "Next time I'd like to tell you about two more hardwoods that are native to our state."

CHAPTER FIFTEEN

"He hath made every thing beautiful in his time."
Ecclesiastes 3:11

Spring Butterflies

"Joel." Ruth looked up from the book she was reading.

"Yes," Joel answered, turning to look at his sister.

"In here it tells how to make a butterfly net." She held up *Spring and Summer in North Carolina Forests*. "Do you think that if Mother helped me with the net you could help me with the handle? I saw a small blue butterfly fluttering around today, and I'd like to be able to catch it. But, you probably have plenty of other things to do today since Father didn't need your help at work."

"I think I can help you anyway, sis." Joel took the book with a smile and studied the directions. "While you get started on the net, I'll hunt up some wire and an old mop handle."

Later that afternoon, Ruth took the net out to the shop to show Joel. "May we get the wire ready now?"

"Sure." He picked up a piece of wire he had cut to the proper length. "This is some wire Father said he doesn't need anymore. But how shall we get it bent into a circle without ending up with an oval?"

"I think I know just the thing." Ruth pointed to a Douglas fir near Father's woodpile.

"That does look as though it will work." Joel handed her the wire. "Just watch for pitch, or you'll get your hands all sticky."

"I will. Thanks, Joel."

An hour later, Ruth found Joel out in the garage. "Here," she said, handing him the wire with the net attached. "Mother helped me sew it on."

"It looks good." He took the net from her.

"Do you have your book?"

Ruth hurried to get it. "Here are the directions." She passed him the open book.

"Let's see." He studied the measurements and bent both ends of the wire accordingly.

Glancing at the book once more, he reached for the drill. "I need to make two grooves part way down the sides of the handle," he told her. "Then I'll make two holes at the end of each groove." He started the drill and ran it down a few inches on both sides of the handle.

"There," he said, drilling two holes at the end of each groove. "Now for the wire." He slipped the wire into the proper holes and slid a hose clamp over the wire to hold it down.

"Now you're all set." Joel playfully swept the net onto Ruth's head.

She ducked out and grabbed the net. "Thank you *very* much!"

"You're very welcome. Just don't catch too many of your brothers!"

Catching butterflies became the subject at the supper table that evening. "Why don't you use the freezer instead of a killing jar." Mother passed the peas to Father. "That might be best for right now. Then you won't have to worry about chemical fumes."

174

"That is fine with me," Ruth agreed. "Do you have some freezer containers you could spare?"

"Yes." Mother nodded. "I'll get them for you after supper. Remember to handle your specimens carefully. In the freezer it is very easy for their antennae or legs to break."

"I'll try to be careful," Ruth assured her.

"I have some mounting blocks you may use," Joel offered. "I haven't used them for several years. I'll even give you some lessons in mounting if you are interested."

"I'd be glad for them." She smiled.

The next day Ruth stood gazing out the window. "Oh, look, Mother. I see a butterfly." She pointed to a fluttering bit of blue among the hemlock branches. "May I go and try to catch it, please?"

"You may try," Mother consented, "but I will be needing your help in the kitchen before too long."

Once outside with her net, Ruth scanned the trees for the butterfly. "There it is," she whispered, cautiously creeping toward it.

Swoosh. She swung her net, but the tiny insect sailed quickly out of reach.

Ruth was disappointed. "This isn't going to

be as easy as I thought," she sighed.

Her eyes caught sight of another butterfly, which was bobbing near some blackberry vines. "Now if I can just . . . " Ruth aimed carefully and soon had a fluttering object in her net.

"Good." Ruth let out a deep breath, and giving the handle a quick half-turn, she closed the opening. "Now to get it into a container. I hope it doesn't tear its wings," she said with concern as it flopped around.

After the butterfly was safely in the freezer, Ruth stepped out into the bright April sunshine again. "Maybe I can catch another one for Joel to help me with when he and Father get home."

Her eyes searched for more butterflies while she paused in the yard a few moments. "Oh, an orange one!" she exclaimed softly as it darted by. "I'll follow it."

It flitted along and then stopped to rest on a blackberry vine, closing its wings.

"Now where is it?" Ruth searched for a glimpse of the orange insect. "Oh, I see it now. Its underwings are brown, so I didn't see it at first. If it will just stay there, I can catch it." She quickly brought the net down.

"Do I have time to catch one more?" Ruth asked Mother when the orange butterfly was in a container. "Then we'll have three to mount tonight."

"You may." Mother smiled as she poured a bowl of cake batter into a pan.

Ruth walked back over to the wild blackberry vines. "Look at all the flowers on this

Satyr anglewing butterfly on blackberry vines

plant," she said, admiring the small white blossoms. "It looks as though it will have a lot more berries than that one by the cedar tree. The flowers on that vine are noticeably smaller."

A white butterfly fluttered by just then, and Ruth was startled out of her musing in time to swing the net. "There. That makes three. Joel will be busy tonight."

After supper, Joel found his mounting equipment. "I'm going to put these butterflies on a napkin." He gingerly shook them out of their containers. "That way their wings won't get wet when the ice on the containers melts.

He picked up a pair of tweezers. "To open their wings you gently pinch them on the abdomen below the wings," he instructed, grasping the blue butterfly with the tweezers. "This makes it easier to slide the insect pin into the abdomen." He slid a pin into the butterfly and placed it on the mounting block.

Spring azure butterfly

"I think this is a spring azure, an early spring butterfly. Why don't you look it up? You'll need to compare the gray markings on the whitish underside with the picture in the book to know for sure. Some of these blues are hard to tell apart."

Ruth carefully studied the picture and the butterfly. "You are right. It is a spring azure—blue with a lavender tint above and grayish

Cabbage white butterfly

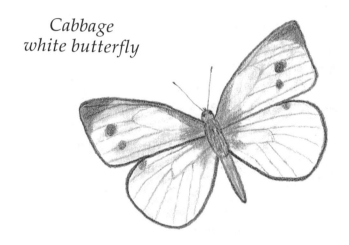

white with darker bars and marks below."

Joel picked up the white butterfly with dark tips on its forewings. "This is a cabbage white. I think it is a female; they have two spots on each forewing. At least you're catching a garden pest for once!"

"Really?" Ruth wondered. "What do they

do? Do they eat cabbage?"

"Yes, their larvae do." Joel spread out its wings. "Their larvae also eat broccoli, kale, and cauliflower. They were introduced from Europe, so they have no God-planned natural controls here. Although you may catch as many cabbage whites as you want, be sparing in collecting the other kinds. A male and a female of each type are enough. As stewards of God's creation, we don't want to take part in destroying an entire kind of butterfly."

"That's right," Father agreed. "The government will permit catching butterflies only if you are sparing. This is wise."

"A-a-cho-o-oo!" Timothy entered the room with a handkerchief over his mouth. "Oh, this is a bad cold," he sighed. "Do you have anything for my throat, Mother?"

Mother reached into the cupboard above the sink. "Try this throat drop and a good night's sleep."

"Thanks." He grinned crookedly.

Father slipped his hand into his pocket. "I forgot to give this to you, Timothy." He tossed him a white envelope. "Looks like another letter from Grandpa Kropf in Pennsylvania."

"Oh, good." Timothy's eyes brightened. He

sat down near Joel.

"Just don't sneeze the butterfly away," Joel teased.

"Hm-mph," Timothy grunted as he slit open the envelope.

"Would you like to do this anglewing, Ruth?" Joel asked as he finished positioning the cabbage white, tacking the wings down with

*Satyr
anglewing
butterfly*

narrow strips of paper.

"No." Ruth smiled. "I think I'll just watch for today. I wouldn't want to ruin it."

"That's fine." Joel carefully pushed the pin into the anglewing. "Do you see the silver commas on its hind wings? They contrast with the rest of its duller tan underside. This is a satyr anglewing."

"It certainly is pretty," Ruth breathed,

watching Joel line the forewings horizontal to the rest of the body.

"Its golden orange upper wings with their black blotches are attractive, aren't they?" Joel agreed.

"Yes." Ruth watched him intently. "But why aren't the underwings as pretty?"

"To help the butterfly hide from predators," Joel replied, placing a strip of paper over the butterfly's right side. "The same great and wise God who cares for us also pays attention to the smallest details of His other creatures. He certainly meets all our needs."

"A-a-cho-o-oo!" Timothy looked up from his letter. "Even by sending me a cheerful letter from Grandpa."

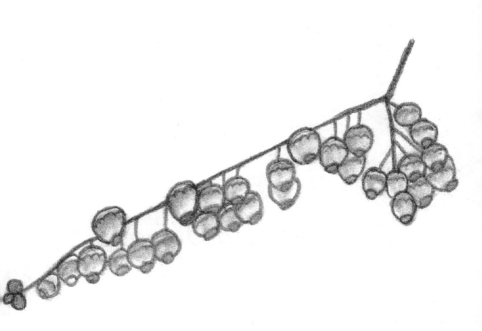

CHAPTER SIXTEEN

"Sing, O ye heavens; for the Lord hath done it: shout, ye lower parts of the earth: break forth into singing, ye mountains, O forest, and every tree therein: for the Lord hath redeemed Jacob, and glorified himself in Israel."

Isaiah 44:23

Two More Hardwoods

"Who is ready to find the object of our next tree lesson?" Father asked one Saturday afternoon in early May.

"We are!" Timothy and Ruth replied eagerly.

"Is it easy to find?" Joel asked.

"If you went out and started looking for it by yourself, it would take awhile." Father smiled. "We only have one on our property that I know of."

"I'll come with you then," Joel said with a grin, untying his shoes and slipping into his rubber boots by the back door.

"We only have one?" Timothy repeated. "I have no idea what it is."

"Nor do I." Ruth began to list the ones she knew. "Douglas fir, hemlock, cedar, red alder, willow—that's all I know of."

"Well, let's go introduce you then." Father held the door open for them and started down the back path that looped through the back part of their wooded acreage.

Pausing at a bend in the trail, he said, "We're almost there. In fact, I can see it from here."

Timothy and Ruth searched the tall timber for something unfamiliar. "I'm stumped," Timothy declared.

"You're setting your sights too high." Father gave a hint. "This tree is still young."

Together they scanned the underbrush. "Is that it?" Ruth pointed. "Is it a maple?"

"That's right." Father smiled. "Let's get a closer look at it. Watch for those mountain beavers.

"The big leaf maple is the only large maple on the West Coast." Father plucked off a shiny green leaf, cut into five deep lobes. "It has the

Big leaf maple

largest leaves of any maple, eight to twelve inches across and ten to twelve inches long."

"Big leaves," Timothy commented. "How tall are big leaf maples, normally?"

"Seventy to eighty feet," Father replied. "But they may be over one hundred feet tall and three to four feet in diameter."

"The bark on the older trees is furrowed with regular or irregular cracks," Joel told them. "This tree is still young." He stroked the smooth gray bark.

"Yes," Father agreed. "Do you remember the large maples that Uncle Peters have?"

"How could I forget?" Timothy grinned. "I was climbing into one of those large, lovely maples and got stung by a bee!"

"They had a nest there," Joel remembered. "You should have checked first."

"I like playing with 'helicopters' from their maples in the fall," Ruth put in.

"Those are maple seeds." Father pointed to a hanging cluster of one-quarter-inch maple flowers in the tree. "And these are the flowers. In a little while, a sticky, golden brown cluster of seeds will be hanging there."

"Then we can come and play with them in the fall," Ruth said, recalling what fun she had

had tossing the hairy, winged seeds into the air and watching them spin to the ground.

"Now we don't have to go to Uncle Peters to do that." Timothy looked up at the twenty-five-foot tree. "We have a maple of our own."

"Maple wood is valued here in the West," Father told them. "We don't have very many hardwoods here. In fact, the big leaf maple is the only commercially important maple on the

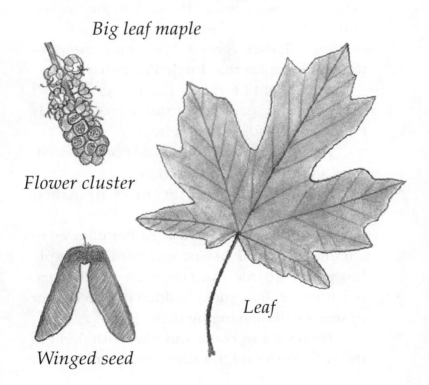

Big leaf maple

Flower cluster

Winged seed

Leaf

entire West Coast."

"What do people do with it?" Timothy wondered.

"It is used to make furniture, woodenware, and veneer," Father answered. "Veneer is a thin layer of maple that is bonded to the top of a material of lesser quality to cover it."

"Weren't you going to tell us about another tree today too?" Ruth wondered. "You said that you would show us two this time."

"I did, didn't I?" Father started back out onto the trail. "Our other tree is also a hardwood, but it is an unusual one. It doesn't lose its leaves in the fall."

"Hm-m-m. Do we have one only of those too?" Timothy questioned.

"Yes, we do." Joel realized where Father was taking them.

Down the lane they strolled. Stopping near the bottom, Father asked, "Who can guess which tree is our next subject?"

"Is it that tree with the dark orange bark?" Timothy guessed.

"Correct," Father replied. "That is a madrone or madrona."

"It looks as if it is losing its bark." Ruth looked worried.

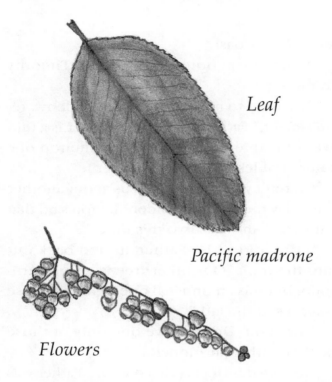

Leaf

Pacific madrone

Flowers

"But that is one of the unusual things about it," Father told her. "Its bark is deciduous. It peels off in the summer, and in the fall new bark takes its place."

"What an interesting tree." Timothy pulled off a thin, cinnamon red strip of bark, exposing the smooth, bright trunk.

"Look above you, Timothy," Father directed. "Do you see the hanging flower clusters?"

"Are they white?" Timothy spotted a clump.

Pacific madrone

"Yes," Father answered. "Later they will have small orange red berries that robins and varied thrushes like to eat."

Buzz. Buzz. A female rufous appeared and began sipping nectar from a white cluster.

"Hummingbirds must like madrone too," Ruth decided, reaching up and plucking off a leathery green leaf. "Don't the leaves look polished?"

"Yes, they do." Joel examined a leaf for himself.

"The madrone is a medium-sized tree," Father told them. "These trees are usually 80 to 125 feet tall."

"It's also our best firewood, isn't it?" Joel asked.

"That's right." Father watched another hummingbird fill up on nectar. "Its wood is soft at first but turns hard and brittle. And maple is our second-best firewood."

"So we studied firewood trees today?" Timothy plucked off a madrone leaf and studied its dull, rough underside.

"Yes." Father nodded. "And this ends your tree lessons from me for now. But God has created many varieties of trees. Keep your eyes open, and you will find many more to study."

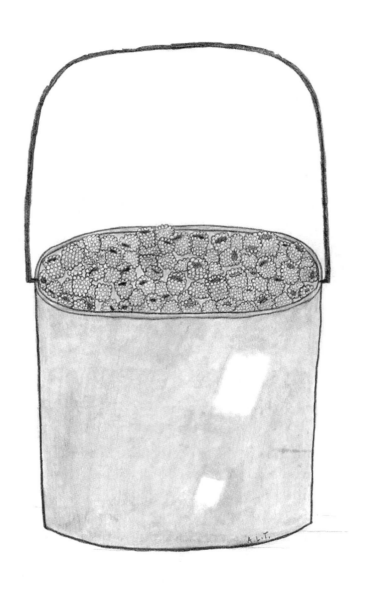

CHAPTER SEVENTEEN

*"For thou, Lord, hast
made me glad through thy
work: I will triumph in the
works of thy hands. O Lord,
how great are thy works!"*
Psalm 92:4, 5

Salmon and Chickenmumps

"Oh, look at these pretty little flowers." Ruth
bent down for a closer look. "They look like
tiny pink bells."

"Those are twinflowers," Mother told her.
"See how each stem is forked to bear a pair of
tiny bells?"

"Yes, I can see why they are called
twinflowers."

"They grow on dainty vines that can carpet

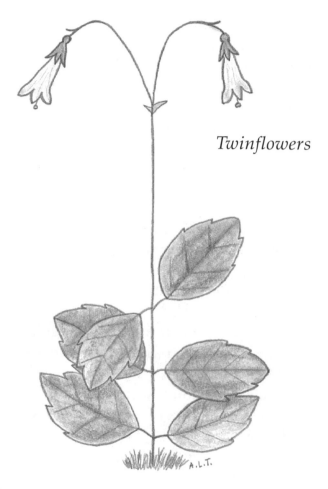

Twinflowers

a large area with their evergreen foliage."
Mother held one up gently.

"They have such tiny leaves," Ruth
remarked, stroking a shiny, toothed leaf. "God
has made so many lovely things."

195

"Aren't you coming?" Timothy and David had unknowingly proceeded down the trail without them. "We would like to see if the salmonberries are ripe."

"Yes. We're coming." They stood to their feet to follow the boys.

As they neared the salmonberry patch, a small dark brown streak dashed out in front of them. "What was that?" David asked excitedly.

The fuzzy little creature paused briefly on a moss-covered log to see who had invaded his territory.

"A chipmunk," Ruth whispered. "See him on that log over there?"

"Oh, I *see* him!" David shouted gleefully.

With that outburst, the chipmunk darted into a thicket of salal.

"You scared him," Ruth said sadly.

"I'm sorry," David cried. "I *do so* love chickenmumps."

"You mean chipmunks, David?" Mother asked kindly.

He nodded vigorously.

Timothy squelched a smile and tried to comfort his brother. "Cheer up, David. We might see him on the way back if we are quiet. If not, when our strawberries are ripe, you'll see one.

They like our strawberries."

"What else do they like, Mother?" David's disappointment began to fade.

"They like other berries too, in the summer. And when it is fall, they will eat nuts, seeds, and underground fungi."

"Fun-gi," David repeated. "What's that?"

"Fungi are a large group of plants like mushrooms," Mother answered. "So chipmunks eat underground mushroomlike plants."

"Oh." David watched as Ruth edged closer to the salal thicket.

"Mother," Ruth said excitedly, "the salal bushes are blooming. Look at all the clusters of round pink bells!"

"There are a lot." Mother came closer. "In a little while, these bushes will have berries."

"Speaking of berries," Timothy said waving his bucket with a grin, "may I go look for salmonberries now?"

"Certainly," Mother replied with a smile. "And we are coming too—as long as we don't stop for any more flowers."

"Oh, look! There are the salmonberries!" The sight of the salmon yellow fruit against the green, saw-toothed leaves made David jump eagerly.

Timothy launched into picking without

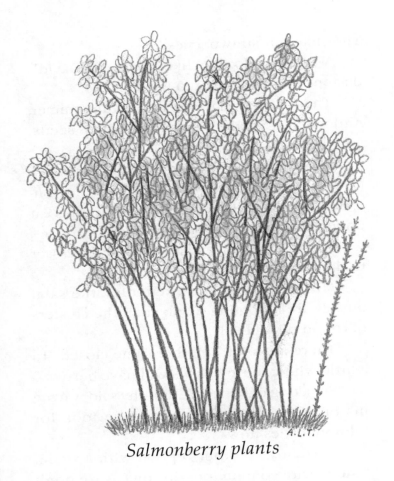

Salmonberry plants

delay. "These are the first berries to ripen, aren't they?"

Mother started filling her bucket. "Yes, next there will be blackberries and huckleberries and thimbleberries and . . . "

"I'm glad God made so many berries!" David managed to say between mouthfuls of the rasp-berry-shaped fruit. "But I think I like black-berries best. These aren't like blackberries."

"No," Mother agreed. "But they will make good jelly."

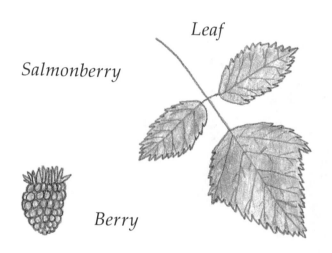

Leaf

Salmonberry

Berry

"Why are they called salmonberries, Mother?" Ruth wondered. "Some of these riper berries are red."

"That is true." Mother put another handful into her pail. "Many of them are salmon-colored though. That could be one reason for

Townsend chipmunk in salal thicket

the name. Another reason that I've heard was that early explorers used salmonberry bark to help their stomachs when they ate too much salmon."

"I didn't know that." Timothy popped a berry into his mouth.

A while later, Mother remarked, "It looks as though we've cleaned this patch of its berries. Shall we go back to the house and make some salmonberry jelly?"

"Yes." David hurried to get one more handful of fruit.

As they walked past the salal thicket, David exclaimed, "I see the chickenmump! I mean chipmunk! He has a salmonberry too!"

The little creature retreated into the thicket at David's exclamation. "I'm so-o-o glad I saw him again!"

A little later Mother stood over the stove, stirring the pot of boiling yellow orange berries. "Is the old pillowcase ready, Ruth? These are ready to be strained."

Ruth hooked the worn pillowcase onto its place by the cupboard. "Now it is." She placed a large bowl under it for catching the juice.

"Please put a hot mat near the bowl." Mother flipped off the burner switch and set the pan down as soon as the hot mat was in place. "Now, if you will hold the pillowcase open, I'll ladle this in."

Ruth watched the honey-colored juice run out through the bottom of the pillowcase. "May I squeeze it after all the berries are in?"

"Perhaps after it cools some." Mother scraped the last of the berries into the case. "It is too hot to squeeze now."

Later Mother was lifting steaming jars of golden orange jelly out of the canner. "It looks good," Ruth commented.

"And tastes good too." Timothy scraped out the pan. "Almost like honey."

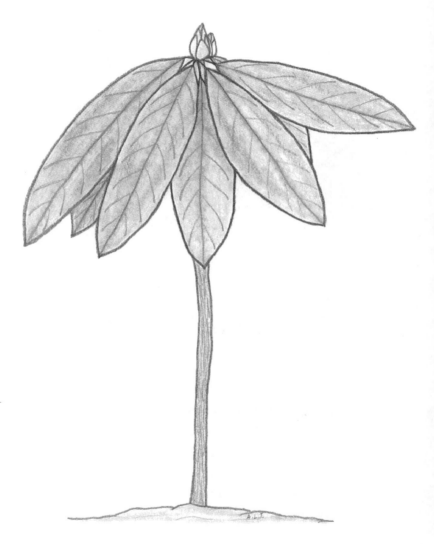

CHAPTER EIGHTEEN

"But ye shall receive power, after that the Holy Ghost is come upon you: and ye shall be witness unto me both in Jerusalem, and in all Judaea, and in Samaria, and unto the uttermost part of the earth."

Acts 1:8

Birthday Surprise

One early June morning, the children gathered around Father in the kitchen. "Won't she be surprised?" Ruth whispered, taking a stack of golden brown pancakes off the griddle.

"Sh-h-h-h," Joel warned as she opened the squeaky oven door. "We don't want to wake Mother yet."

"Where are we going after breakfast?" Timothy spread tuna fish salad on the slices of bread before him. "A picnic will be fun."

"I'll let that be a surprise for you," Father said with a smile, turning the bacon over.

"What are you doing?" David pattered into the kitchen, rubbing his eyes.

"Sh-h-h-h." Ruth held her finger to her lips.

"Why?" David asked loudly.

Joel swooped him into his arms. "Let's get you dressed, little man. We have a busy day ahead of us."

Shortly after Joel and David returned, Mother entered the kitchen. "Well, well, what is going on in here?"

"Happy birthday!" Timothy grinned as he bagged the last sandwich.

"Why, thank you. I had forgotten all about it." Mother peered over Father's shoulder. "I see you have breakfast well in hand."

"Are you ready to eat?" Father asked her. "I'd like to get an early start today."

"Certainly," Mother replied. "But we don't need to go anywhere special on my account."

"But we *want* to." Joel led Mother to her place at the table. "Please have a seat, and breakfast will be served."

Mother laughed. "You must really want me to take it easy today!"

Half an hour later, Father closed the car door and put the key in the ignition. "Let's bow our heads in prayer before we start.

"Our heavenly Father, we thank You for bringing us to another day. We ask that You would please bless Mother on her birthday. We pray for safety as we travel, according to Your will. Please help us to be faithful, consistent witnesses for You. May Your will be done in all of this. In Jesus' Name. Amen."

Buckling his safety belt, he said, "Now we are ready to go." Father started the car and drove out the lane.

"Where are we going?" David asked eagerly.

"You will soon find out." Father looked both ways and pulled onto the road.

In several minutes, they approached the Hood Canal Floating Bridge. "Oh, good. I like going across the bridge." Ruth craned her neck to see it. "Let's see if we can hold our breath all the way across."

"Whew-w-w," the children all sighed at the same time.

"We didn't quite make it." Ruth giggled as they neared the end of the longest salt-water floating bridge in the world. "Maybe if it were shorter than a mile we could have done it."

Hood Canal Bridge

Before long they were southbound on Highway 101. "Oh," Mother said, "now I know where we are going. That would be a good birthday present."

"Oh, Whitney Rhododendron Gardens!" Ruth exclaimed as they pulled into the parking lot. "I really like it here. June is just the right time to see the rhododendrons in bloom."

"Thank you, Father," Mother said as she opened her door. "This is a pleasant surprise."

"So many pretty colors," Ruth said with delight as they strolled among the evergreen foliage. "Lavender, pink, orange, yellow, red . . . "

"Look at that one!" David pointed to a twenty-five-foot rhododendron. "It looks like a tree!"

"You're right," Father agreed. "Usually the ones we see are four to eight feet high, but they may grow as large as a small tree."

"Oh, I like this one." Ruth bent over a cluster of lavender flowers. "The deep purple centers accent the lavender so well."

"*Rhododendron* is such a long name," Timothy remarked. "What does it mean?"

"It is a combination of two Greek words," Mother answered. *"Rhodon* meaning 'rose' and *dendron* meaning 'tree.' In other words, a rose tree."

"Interesting." Joel felt a stiff, leathery leaf from a red-flowered plant.

"The leaves seem almost brittle, don't they?" Mother watched him feel the oblong leaf.

"Did you know rhododendrons are poisonous?" Father asked them.

"I think I've heard that before," replied

Rhododendron

Timothy, stepping into a greenhouse where young plants were growing. "Do these come from seeds?"

"I believe they are started from cuttings," Mother told him.

Father pulled his watch out of his pocket. "It's almost dinnertime. Why don't we finish looking here and then go to a park to eat."

After they finished dinner, Mother packed the leftover food into the cooler. "Thank you all so much for such an enjoyable birthday. I've had a wonderful time."

"We're not done yet." Father carried the cooler and the picnic basket to the car. "I have one more surprise for you."

"Really?" Mother laughed softly. "Haven't I had enough surprises?"

"No, not yet." Timothy climbed into the waiting car.

A woman hurried over to their car just before the rest got in. "Excuse me." She approached Mother. "I couldn't help noticing your family. What religion are you?"

"We are Christians who believe in following the Bible," Mother replied simply.

"Well, I knew *that* already." The woman smiled. "But what *are* you?"

"People call us Mennonites."

"Oh, okay. I know what those are." She tossed her stylish hair back over her shoulder. "Somewhat like the Amish."

Mother nodded. "Yes, we are similar. "But a name is not what matters. Obedience to the Bible, the Word of God, is what's most important."

"Yes, yes." The woman nodded vigorously. "Thanks for taking the time to talk with me. I just thought I'd come and ask. Keep it up. We're all watching you."

"Would you like some more information about what we believe?" Mother asked.

"Sure." The woman took the tract Mother offered and turned to go. "Thank you."

"There is someone else to pray for," Father remarked as Mother climbed into the car beside him. "We never know when the Lord will give us the opportunity to witness for Him."

"Did you notice she said people are watching us?" Joel asked.

"Yes," Father replied. "That is why it is so important to walk carefully. Of ourselves, we cannot be good witnesses for the Lord, but when He empowers us, we are able to do all things for His glory."

Soon they were on the highway once more. "Where are we going now?" Mother wondered as they turned onto a gravel road.

"To get a present for you," Father answered mysteriously.

"I don't know what it would be." Mother was puzzled.

Father pulled to a stop in a wild rhododendron thicket at the end of the road. "Here we are." He smiled. "Which plant do you want? I have permission from the timber company to dig a few."

"Now I know what my present is!" Mother smiled in appreciation.

"I wondered what the pots and the shovel were for." Ruth hopped out.

"This looks like a good one." Mother picked out a three-foot bush with a few pink blossoms.

"I think it's a very good choice." Father proceeded to dig it up.

"Why are they all pink?" David wondered. "Aren't there any yellow ones? I like yellow."

"These are wild rhododendrons, David," Father explained. "Their flowers are a rosy pink. The many-colored ones we saw today were made by crossing different plants to get special colors."

"Oh, Father," Ruth called. "Here is a small rhododendron. May I have it?" She stood beside a one-foot stalk with only one cluster of leaves.

"I don't know how it will do." Father came over after he had potted Mother's plant. "But we certainly can try. It might do quite well."

"Thank you, Father." Ruth watched as he dug up the small bush.

"Yes, thank you." Mother joined them. "I have enjoyed this day tremendously."

CHAPTER NINETEEN

"O Lord God of hosts, who is a strong Lord like unto thee? or to thy faithfulness round about thee? Thou rulest the raging of the sea: when the waves thereof arise, thou stillest them."

Psalm 89:8, 9

Uncle Elmer's Sea

"I think it will suit us just fine, Grandfather," Father said into the receiver. "I'll talk to Ellen and see. The children would enjoy that."

Everyone was looking at Father with curious expressions when he hung up the telephone. Father smiled broadly. "That was Grandfather. He just got a call from Uncle Elmer. He told Grandfather that he would really like for us to come and see him this week.

Grandfather feels it is urgent. Uncle Elmer may be seeking the Lord again."

"Oh, that *is* good news." Joel brightened. "Lately I have been praying for him often."

"It would suit me to go," Mother said thoughtfully. "With all these good helpers, we can be ready to leave tomorrow, I believe."

"That's exactly what Grandfather suggested." Father nodded. "I'll call Grandfather back right now. Then let's get busy packing. If Uncle Elmer is seeking the Lord, we want to go as soon as we can."

Relief shone in Uncle Elmer's eyes as the now-familiar station wagon appeared in his clearing. "Hello, hello, everyone! It's so good to see you again. Did Grandfather tell you that I'd like to take you to the ocean tomorrow? I so much enjoy living near the ocean. That was one of the reasons I moved here." Suddenly a dark cloud passed over his face.

"I would really, really like to see the ocean, Uncle Elmer," David told him. "And I'm glad to see you again too. Please don't look so sad."

Uncle Elmer smiled down at David. "Did I look sad, my boy?"

After the others had gone to bed, Uncle Elmer and Grandfather were still sitting outside at the picnic table talking.

"Let's pray for Uncle Elmer and Grandfather, boys," Father said, kneeling beside his cot.

And many more prayers were raised for Uncle Elmer that night.

The next morning, David bounced into the main room of Uncle Elmer's cabin. "Today we see the ocean." He looked happily into Uncle Elmer's face.

"Why, Uncle Elmer," David said with an even bigger smile, "you look like you know God again! You look very happy."

Uncle Elmer smiled broadly down at him. "Praise the Lord, I do, my boy."

David clapped his hands. "Oh, good. We prayed and prayed for you for ever so long."

Tears came to Uncle Elmer's eyes. "I'm surely thankful you did, David; that I am."

*　　　*　　　*　　　*　　　*

The wind whipped around the eager group as they plodded along a grass-lined trail that led to the beach. "This grass has sharp edges." Timothy felt a blade as he mounted the crest of a sand dune.

"Yes, be careful with it," Father warned.

218

"Sand is hard to walk in," David puffed. "Are we almost there?"

"Here we are now!" Uncle Elmer announced joyfully.

"It's beautiful," Ruth whispered as they topped the last dune and caught a full view of the waves rising and breaking on the sandy shore.

"It's *big*," David said with wide-eyed amazement. "Very, very big."

"Yes, it is," Father agreed. "'O Lord, how manifold are thy works! in wisdom hast thou made them all: the earth is full of thy riches.'"

"'So is this great and wide sea'"—Uncle Elmer remembered the next verse—"'Wherein are things creeping innumerable, both small and great beasts.'"

"'There go the ships.'" Joel quoted part of the next verse, pointing to a cargo ship on the distant horizon.

"Oh, Grandmother, look at these." Ruth motioned to some trailing vines at her feet. "Their yellow flower clusters are so pretty." She reached down and touched the stem. "Oh, they're sticky."

"It is the yellow sand verbena," Grandmother told her. "It is one of the most colorful

Yellow sand verbena

flowers on our beaches."

"Why are they sticky, Grandmother?" David grasped one of the thick, fleshy leaves.

"Perhaps that is the way God planned to protect their tender vines." Grandmother bent over slowly and sniffed a fragrant flower head. "They collect enough sand to double their weight, which helps to anchor them in turbulent ocean winds."

David flopped down on the warm sand. "May I go barefoot?"

"You may," Father consented. "Just watch your step, and don't get your clothes wet."

"May I too, please?" Timothy asked with pleading eyes.

At Father's nod, he soon rid himself of shoes and stockings and went running down the beach after David.

David came to an abrupt stop not far away, and Timothy almost collided into him. "What is this, Timothy?" he wondered, picking up a whitish, round object. "An old pancake?"

"A sand dollar." Timothy shivered a little as a gust of wind swept around him.

David held it so that Timothy could get a better look. "Is it one dollar or two?"

Timothy grinned. "It's only one dollar, but we don't use sand dollars for money." He took the flat three-inch shell from David to study it closer. "Let's go ask Uncle Elmer about your 'dollar.'"

Timothy and David ran back to Uncle Elmer. "Can you please tell us about sand dollars?"

"Well," said Uncle Elmer, rubbing his chin. "Sand dollars are related to sea urchins, those spiny pincushions you see in tide pools. This

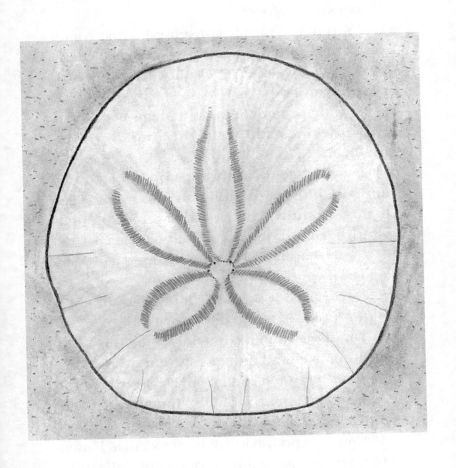

Sand dollar

is really just a sand dollar skeleton. Live sand dollars are covered with many small purple brown spines, which give them a soft appearance."

David looked at the sand dollar. "This is *really* dead then. He has no hair at all. But at least he still has a flower on his back."

"The flower on his back is actually a pattern of tiny holes," Uncle Elmer told him. "Didn't the Lord give sand dollars a pretty design?"

"Yes." David nodded vigorously, stroking the rough shell.

"Boys," Father called, "why don't you get your shoes and socks back on. That wind is getting cold." Father bent down to help David scrape the sand off his feet.

"Do you see that man farther down the beach, Uncle Elmer?" Timothy asked as he pulled on a shoe. "What is he doing?"

Uncle Elmer squinted for a better look. "I think he is fishing, likely for sea perch. Shall we walk down there and see if he has caught anything?

"Did you catch any fish yet?" Uncle Elmer asked when the man with brown chest waders was within hearing distance.

"Not yet. I'm having some competition." He

Fisherman with pile perch

turned to smile at the group. "Did you see that harbor seal a few minutes ago?"

"No, we didn't," replied Father, looking out across the white-tipped waves.

"Well, keep your eyes open. You might see him yet. Just look for a small gray head peeking out of the waves. They are pretty little animals, but they enjoy my sea perch!"

Harbor seal

"We'll watch for him," Uncle Elmer said with a nod.

"Why did he have those funny overalls on?" David whispered as they walked away.

"So he will stay dry when he wades out into the water," Father answered. "They are called chest waders."

"Oh." David glanced back at the man again. "Oh! Oh! Oh! Look at him back there! He's

225

catching something!"

"Good," Joel said, turning to look. "I hoped that he would while we are watching him."

The man noticed their glances and held up a spiny little fish for them to see before dropping it into his bucket.

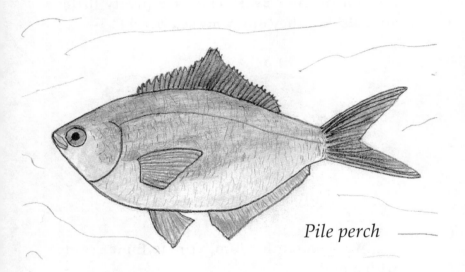

Pile perch

"Is that a seal?" Ruth asked suddenly, pointing to a dark head bobbing in the waves not far from the beach.

"Yes, it is." Uncle Elmer saw it too. "What a special treat to see one."

The dark head disappeared and popped up farther from the shore. "There he is again,"

Joel said. "I wonder if he is watching us."

"May I build a sand castle?" David wondered.

"Yes, you may," Father consented. "I'll help you." He bent down and began packing the wet sand together.

"Let's make it enormous." Timothy said as he and Joel joined them.

A bit later, David said happily, "We're almost done now. But, look. The ocean is coming to get it!" David watched the waves with concern in his blue eyes. "I don't want it to!"

"But there is nothing we can do about it," Father told him kindly. "When we build on the sand, the waves come along and wash our buildings away, just like the foolish man in Jesus' parable."

"Then I am a foolish man!" David exclaimed. "I built my house on the sand, and a big storm is coming. I must build my next house on a rock."

"'The wise man built his house upon a rock . . . '" Joel started the familiar tune.

David stood back as the first wave reached the castle. Soon another came, and another. "'And the house on the sand fell *flat*,'" he sang loudly as the castle disappeared under the waves.

Later as they sat enjoying a picnic dinner on the beach, Uncle Elmer said thoughtfully, "You know, I was like that foolish man once. I didn't build my life on the Rock of Salvation, Jesus Christ. But, thank the Lord, He saved my soul, and now I am building upon the Rock. He cast all my sins into the sea of His forgetfulness and made me a new creature in Him. That's the best sea I've ever heard of!"

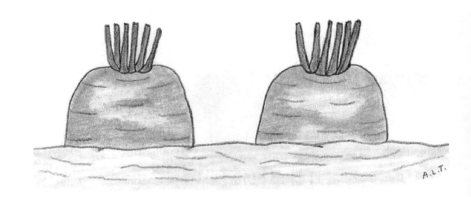

CHAPTER TWENTY

"Great and marvellous are thy works, Lord God Almighty; just and true are thy ways, thou King of saints."

Revelation 15:3

Carrot Tops and Butterflies

Ruth stood quietly at the edge of the front flower bed. "I do hope a butterfly comes soon." She held her net in readiness.

"Oh, a red admiral!" she softly exclaimed as the black butterfly, banded in scarlet and spotted with white, sucked nectar from a pink carnation.

Aiming carefully, she swung the net over the carnation. Too late!

"I missed," she sighed, starting in pursuit of the darting figure.

Into the garden it flitted with Ruth close behind. "Oh, it's going over by my garden patch."

The colorful butterfly stopped to rest on a tall carrot top.

"Now," Ruth thought as she approached, "if it won't be too quick this time. Just a little closer—Why . . . what . . . what happened here?" She gazed at her row of carrots in dismay. "Something ate the tops off half of my carrots! What would have done that?"

Red admiral butterfly

Red admiral forgotten, she dashed into the house. "Mother," she panted, "something ate the tops off half of my carrots! Can you come and see?"

"Yes." Mother put down the potato she was peeling and rinsed her hands.

"Come, David." She wiped her hands on her apron.

"What's going on?" Timothy strode into the kitchen, book in hand.

"Something has been eating my carrot tops," Ruth told him, reaching for the doorknob. "Do you want to come and see too?"

"Of course." He laid his book down and followed them out into the warm summer sunshine.

Once in the garden, they looked for signs from the mysterious carrot eater. "It's hard to tell what it was." Timothy searched the ground for tracks. "Our paths are so well beaten down."

"I know," Ruth sighed. "I just hope it doesn't come and eat the rest of them, whatever it is."

"Don't you want it to come back so you can see it?" Timothy teased. "I do."

"I suppose," Ruth said slowly. "But not at the expense of my carrots!"

Later that afternoon, David stood looking

out the bedroom window. "Mother! Mother! Come quickly, please! There's a deer in the garden. And—and it's eating my baby apple tree!"

Mother hurried to his side. "So it is."

Turning, she called, "Timothy! Ruth! Come and see what ate Ruth's carrots!"

Beating footsteps were heard, and the pair appeared in the bedroom. "What is it?" they chorused, hurrying to the window.

"It's eating my tree!" David cried.

"A deer." Timothy caught sight of the graceful creature.

"Oh, isn't she beautiful?" Ruth said, watching as the deer walked daintily over to the cherry tree and began eating.

"Not my cherries!" David tapped the window loudly to scare her. "She'll eat all our cherries that were soon going to be ready for me to pick and eat!"

The doe lifted timid, frightened black eyes to the house and bounded into the gully, black tail swishing from side to side.

"You must not get so upset, David." Mother put her arm around his shoulder. "She won't eat all our cherries."

"We do need to make sure she stays out of the garden though, don't we?" Ruth asked, her

Columbia black-tailed deer

voice filled with concern.

"Yes, we do," Mother agreed. "We'll have to watch for her. She could do a lot of damage to the garden."

"What kind of deer is she?" Timothy wondered.

"She is a Columbia black-tailed deer," replied Mother. "A subspecies of the mule deer."

Ruth glanced at the forest where the doe had disappeared. "Oh, look." She pointed to the cherry tree. "A swallowtail butterfly. May I go catch it, Mother? I don't have one of them in my collection yet."

"Go ahead," Mother consented.

Soon Ruth was following the flitting butterfly. "It has landed on our lavender rhododendron." Ruth crept along cautiously.

One well-aimed swing had the swallowtail in her net.

"Mother," she said as she put the beautiful insect in a container. "If it's all right with you, I think I'll go look for more butterflies in the horse pasture. I often see them there."

"That is fine with me." Mother pulled two loaves of fresh, steaming bread out of the oven. "After that you may help me make supper."

"All right." Ruth opened the back door. "I'll try to hurry back."

After standing in the pasture a few minutes, Ruth spotted a white form fluttering among the underbrush at the far side of the pasture. "What kind of butterfly is that?" She hurried over to catch it.

The butterfly paused on a blackberry flower and folded its wings. "Its wings are almost clear," Ruth whispered, skillfully bringing the net down. "I want to show this one to Joel."

As Father and Joel walked into the house that evening after work, David rushed over to them. "It—it—it ate mine apple tree!" he burst out. "It truly did." He had forgotten proper English in his anxiety.

"Wait just a minute," Father said calmly. "What ate your tree?"

"A—a—a deer," he stuttered.

"A deer?" Joel raised his eyebrows.

"Yes." Timothy came over to help explain. "A deer. A deer was feeding on his little apple tree and he is worried about it."

"Oh." Father ran his fingers through David's brown hair. "I'm sorry about that, son. She must have thought it was tasty."

"Yes, she did. And she ate Ruth's tops too." David looked up at him.

"Do you mean my carrots' tops?" Ruth asked him kindly.

"Yes, your carrot tops." He nodded his head.

"Oh, Joel," Ruth said, remembering the butterflies, "I caught two more butterflies today. Can you help me mount them after supper?"

"I would be glad to." He smiled.

"And, David," Father said, laying his hand on David's shoulder, "we'll just have to keep a close eye on that apple tree of yours. If the deer eats more of it, I will build a little fence around it."

"Oh, thank you." David beamed. "Then my apple tree will be safe from that deer."

After the supper dishes were cleared away, Ruth carefully shook the transparent butterfly onto a napkin. "Look at this one, Joel. Do you know what it is?"

"Oh, that's a Parnassian. Aren't they pretty? Did you notice their red and black spots?"

Ruth watched Joel pin it to the mounting

Clodius parnassian butterfly

block and position its wings. "No, I didn't."

"This is a Clodius Parnassian," Joel decided after studying it. "We also have a Phoebus Parnassian, but they have two red spots on each forewing. This one does not."

"Ruth," Mother said as she walked over to the pair. "Did you know that Parnassians are related to swallowtails? Both are members of the family *Papilionidae*."

"So I caught two relatives today." Ruth grinned.

"Yes, you did." Mother smiled.

Joel handed Ruth the butterfly field guide before he picked up the swallowtail. "Why don't you see if you can figure out what type of swallowtail this is."

Ruth began flipping through it. "Here it is," she said after comparing the picture and the insect. "An anise swallowtail. The book says they are black with broad yellow bands. I guess that's right, but it looks more yellow to me. It is more black than a tiger swallowtail though."

"Are you ready to try spreading one?" Joel wondered. "A swallowtail is big and easy."

"I know." Ruth watched him poke a pin through the swallowtail's abdomen. "But I don't want to ruin it. It is my first swallowtail

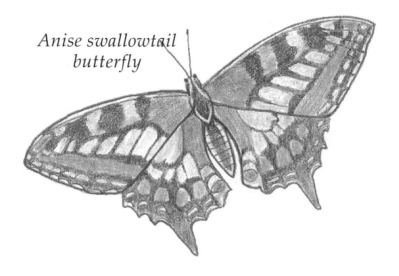

Anise swallowtail butterfly

butterfly, you know."

Joel smiled. "You should catch a cabbage white to practice on. Then you wouldn't worry so much about ruining one."

"So I should concentrate on catching cabbage whites tomorrow?"

"I think so." Joel nodded. "If I keep mounting all your butterflies, you won't get any practice."

"I can always learn by watching," Ruth said with a twinkle in her blue eyes. "But I had better practice so David can learn from me!"

239

CHAPTER
TWENTY-ONE

"I know all the fowls of the mountains: and the wild beasts of the field are mine."
Psalm 50:11

Waxy Wings

"Look, Timothy," Ruth said pointing to a treelike shrub along the back trail, "the red elderberries have fruit on them now."

Timothy observed the clusters of tiny scarlet berries set against groups of green, oblong leaves. "Pretty, but unlike the blue elderberries, they're poisonous."

"Yes." Ruth plucked off a round red berry and threw it into the bushes. "I hope David remembers that. We'll have to remind him."

"I think he knows he should ask before he eats anything," Timothy said. "Right, Mother?" he called back to her.

"Eats what?" Mother and David approached the pair.

"David knows he's not to eat a berry without asking, doesn't he?" Timothy wondered.

"Oh, yes," David answered for himself. "And those berries beside Ruth are not good!

"I'm glad that you know that." Mother laid her hand on his shoulder. "But always remember to ask. God has created many types of berries, but some are not for us to eat."

David nodded. "I know. Those bushes beside Ruth even smell like they are bad for me; they stink!"

"Oh, look!" Ruth exclaimed softly as they rounded a bend in the trail near the horse pasture. "Look at those birds on those elderberry bushes."

Everyone stopped short.

The flock of light brown birds perched quietly on the tall shrub.

"They look so soft." David remembered to whisper.

"Do you see that one?" Timothy squinted

for a better look. "It has a shiny red spot on each wing."

"Oh, yes," Ruth said with a nod. "With their crests and black faces, they look like small, multicolored cardinals."

"I want to see!" David forgot to speak softly this time.

A whir of wings was heard, and the flock vanished into the dense evergreens.

"I wonder what kind of birds they were," Ruth said as the group began moving again.

"I'd like to know too." Mother guided David around a mountain beaver hole. "They were beautiful birds."

Back at the house, Ruth skimmed her bird guide to find the mysterious birds. "I found them. They were waxwings."

"Really?" Mother looked over her shoulder. "Then they must have been cedar waxwings. They had yellowish bellies."

"You're right," Ruth agreed.

"Waxwing?" echoed Timothy, coming over to them. "What a strange name."

"But you were the one to first discover the 'wax.'" Ruth pointed to the red on their wings. "Those red spots are waxlike."

"Well, what do those waxy birds eat?" he

Cedar waxwing on red elderberry

wondered. "Cedar?"

"No." Mother smiled, looking up from a bird book she had pulled off the shelf. "This book says that they eat mostly fruit and also some insects."

"Would they eat elderberries?" Timothy wondered. "They are poisonous to us."

"I'm not sure," Mother replied. "They were in an elderberry bush, but that doesn't mean they were eating elderberries. We'll have to watch them more closely next time."

Timothy had looked them up in another book. "David, listen to this. Another name for the waxwing is cherry bird."

"Cherry bird?" David scratched his head. "Would *they* eat *my* cherries?"

"I'm afraid so," Mother answered. "They are quite fond of cherries. But this is the first time we've seen them, so they may not come and find your cherries."

"Yes. Their habit is to wander from place to place to find fruit," Ruth added. "So they will probably wander somewhere else, since you scared them."

"I hope so." David went back to his blocks. "I don't want those waxes or that deer to eat all my tasty cherries!"

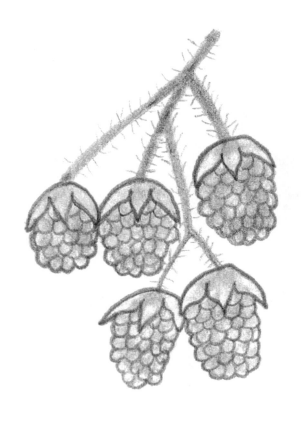

CHAPTER
TWENTY-TWO

"Bless the Lord, O my soul, and forget not all his benefits . . . who satisfieth thy mouth with good things."
Psalm 103:2, 5

Blackberries!

"Children," said Father one Saturday in late June, "the wild blackberries are ripe now. I thought we could pick a few gallons for Mother today. Then we can have blackberry pies this winter."

"Sounds delicious to me." Timothy rubbed his stomach.

"What about jelly or jam?" Ruth wondered. "I like blackberry jam."

"Later this summer, the Himalaya black-berries will ripen. They make good jam," Mother told her. "And these small, wild berries make better pies than the Himalaya berries do."

"All right," Ruth said cheerfully as she went to find her sunbonnet.

Father handed each of them a bucket. "Let's get busy. We want to pick as many berries as we can today. We might not have another opportunity. We want to help Uncle Elmer move next week."

Timothy grinned broadly. "I just can hardly wait until he's moved closer to us. Will he be in our church service tomorrow morning?"

"The Lord willing," Father said with a nod. "I appreciate his willingness to drive a few hours each weekend so he can fellowship with other believers."

"And I am glad to see him." David beamed. "And my uncle Elmer is moving just down the road from us!" He hopped around, clapping his hands.

Father smiled. "It is an answer to prayer that he came back to the Lord. And now are my berry pickers ready to get started? We should try to get our picking done today."

"I know where I'm going to start picking,"

Ruth said, heading for the vine that had had so many big flowers on it that spring. "When I was hunting for butterflies, I found a vine that was loaded with blossoms."

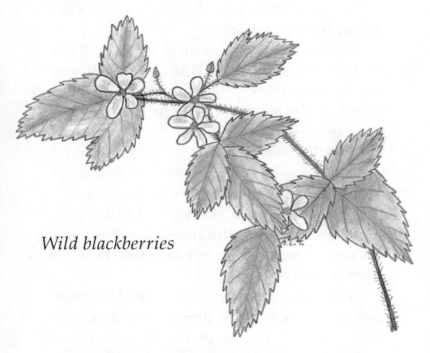

Wild blackberries

Mother and David followed her, with buckets in hand.

"Why—" Ruth stopped short. "This has no berries on it at all. What happened?"

"Maybe that is the wrong vine." Mother began picking on a plant not far away. "There are a number of vines around here."

"I'm sure this was it." Ruth moved to another vine. "I took special notice of it. But I could be wrong," she decided hesitantly.

Father led the boys down the back trail. "There's a good patch on the edge of the property. We should get several quarts off it."

"It also has stinging nettles." Timothy glanced warily at the tall, hairy stalks as they neared the patch. "I'll have to watch for them."

Soon they were joined by the others. "For some people who aren't tired of picking," Mother remarked, smiling at David's purple-splotched face, "and also eating, I'd like a gallon or so of red huckleberries to use in muffins occasionally. But they don't have to be picked today."

"All right." Joel slipped another handful of dark berries into his pail.

"These are poky." David shook his hands. "I get poked when I get my berries."

"Try not to touch the vines," Mother instructed. "If you reach carefully around them, you won't get poked so much."

"Okay." David plucked off another soft, ripe berry and popped it into his mouth.

"They look very much like long, thin

raspberries," Ruth commented. "But their centers aren't hollow. They're solid."

"I got stung again." Joel rubbed his ankle.

"I haven't once." Timothy moved to another group of vines. "I—whoa!" He tripped over a vine. "Ouch! I *had* been watching where I was going."

"'An haughty spirit [goeth] before a fall,' Timothy," Father reminded him. "You should not be boastful."

"I'm sorry." Timothy stood to his feet. "I have been learning the hard way about boasting—with slugs and blackberry vines as my teachers."

"Father." Ruth had been thinking. "I saw a blackberry vine covered with flowers this spring. I took special note of it so I could pick from it later. But it had no fruit on it today. What happened?"

Father smiled. "I think I know. Blackberries have separate male and female vines. The male vines have larger, more noticeable flowers, but they bear no fruit."

"Oh." Ruth laughed. "You can't always tell by appearance, can you? They certainly had me fooled."

"Next time look for the vines with the

smaller flowers," Father told her. "They shouldn't disappoint you."

"It's almost dinnertime, isn't it?" Mother glanced at the position of the sun. "It looks as though we have plenty of blackberries. Why don't we stop for today?"

"Good!" Timothy stretched his arms wide and took a step forward. "Here I go again . . . " He was seen disappearing behind a clump of vines.

"Guess what." He sat up. "I found a mountain beaver hole."

"You must be growing," Joel teased. "You seem to be falling a lot. You need to get used to your longer legs."

Timothy stood up with a chuckle. "Yes. They're just long enough to get my foot in the mountain beaver's burrow!"

David, who had run down the trail ahead of the rest, called back, "May I eat this berry?"

"Let me see." Father took it. "It is a thimbleberry. Yes, you may eat it."

"Thimbleberries are interesting," remarked Joel. "Their leaves look like saw-toothed big leaf maple leaves, and their berries look like flat red raspberries."

"And they are juicy!" David added red berry

Thimbleberry

juice to his numerous purple stains.

"Their flowers look as if they were made of tissue paper," stated Mother, remembering the one- to two-inch flowers she had seen earlier in the year.

"Are you sure you don't want thimbleberry pies instead of blackberry pies?" Ruth teased

Father. "Thimbleberries don't have thorns."

"I wouldn't mind trying it." He grinned. "But I think I'll stick to my blackberry vines, thank you."

After dinner, Joel nudged Timothy. "Let's go get those huckleberries. Father doesn't have much for me to do this afternoon, and I'd rather get them picked now. We can help clean blackberries when we're done."

"Did you ask him?" Timothy preferred to put off the task as long as possible. "The others might need our help cleaning berries now."

"I did, and he said we could go and pick." Joel grabbed two pails. "Let's get this done."

"It takes so-o-o long." Timothy followed reluctantly.

"Cheer up, Timothy. This way you won't

Red huckleberry

Thimbleberries

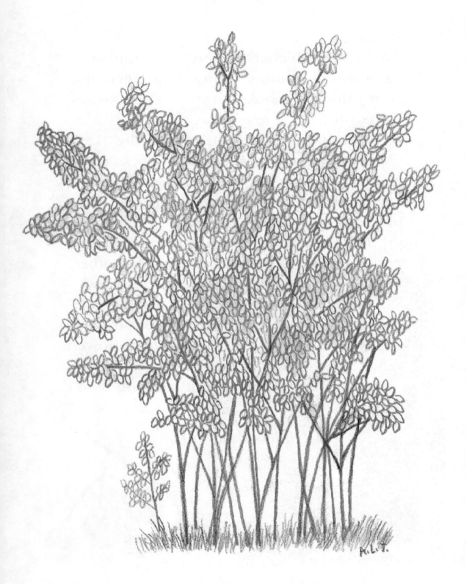

Red huckleberries

have to face small, round berries after we move Uncle Elmer."

"Okay." He took his bucket from Joel. "I'll just see black *and* red berries in my sleep tonight!"

"That's fine." Joel approached a bush with tiny, oblong leaves. "Just as long as we get this

Red huckleberries

Berries

Leaves

job done. If you don't grumble, it will go faster."

"You're right," Timothy admitted, plopping round red berries into his bucket. "Sorry for being so glum."

Joel dropped a few huckleberries into his mouth. "They aren't exactly sweet, but they taste good in baking."

"I like huckleberry muffins." Timothy popped a berry into his mouth. "But I like them plain too, even if they are a little tart."

"So do I." Joel moved to another bush, which was growing out of a rotting cedar stump. "This bush has lots of fruit, but it still takes a while to get two gallons. I have about a cup so far."

"Me too." Timothy peered into his pail. "If I just keep thinking of muffins . . . " He wiped the sweat from his brow.

A while later, Mother had two full pails of huckleberries. "Thank you, boys." She smiled. "I really appreciate your work. Why don't you take a break before you help us clean berries. We're nearly done with the blackberries."

"Thanks." Joel poured a glass of lemonade and sank into a chair. "It's rather warm out there."

"What a full day!" Ruth started sorting huckleberries. "We have lots of berries now."

"Yes," Father agreed. "We need to thank the Lord for all the many blessings He has showered upon us."

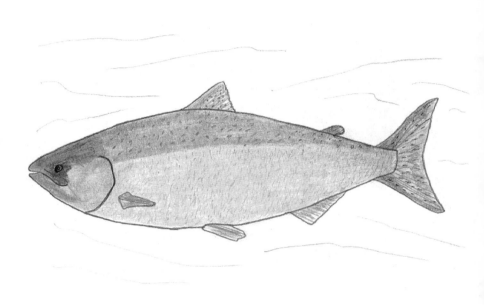

CHAPTER
TWENTY-THREE

"The fishes of the sea shall declare unto thee. Who knoweth not in all these that the hand of the Lord hath wrought this?"

Job 12:8, 9

Fishers of Men

"You know what Uncle Elmer told me?" David asked on the way home from church the next day. "He said he was going to have everything packed and cleaned so all we have to do is load his things."

"I see." Father smiled. "I did hear he has some plans for us tomorrow. He wants to take us to some special place tomorrow and then move his things on Tuesday. I do hope he saves

260

something more than loading for us to do though. We are going to help him, not to go sightseeing."

"Maybe he will take us to the ocean again." David's eyes sparkled happily. "I'd like to find another dollar."

The next morning David was knocking loudly at the cabin door. At Uncle Elmer's "Come in," he burst into the house. "Are we going to the ocean today, Uncle Elmer?" he asked excitedly.

"Not quite," Uncle Elmer said, smiling broadly. "We're going visiting today. How would you like to go to a fishing town?"

"Oh, good." David clapped his hands. "I like fish very much."

Once everyone else had found a place to sit among the boxes, Uncle Elmer explained, "I have some friends—George and Hettie Roberts—who live by Sekiu. I've had a real burden for their souls lately and would like to see them again before I move. So shall we see if the Lord can use us as fishers of men in the fishing town of Sekiu today?"

All heads nodded in agreement.

"Let's pray before we go," Grandfather suggested, bowing his head.

Later that morning they pulled up to an old, dilapidated cabin. The moss-covered porch sagged to one side and the weather-beaten siding had little trace of paint remaining. The door creaked open and a robust elderly man appeared. "Elmer, so good to see you! What brings you here?"

Uncle Elmer shook his hand warmly. "I'm moving back to where my brother lives, and I wanted to say good-bye. But now I should introduce you to this carload." Uncle Elmer flashed them an encouraging smile.

"Come in. Come in," Mrs. Roberts' voice invited from the doorway. "Nice to meet you all." She led the way to the sitting room.

Timothy's eyes widened when he saw the huge fish mounted above the fireplace. "Mr. Roberts," he asked politely, "is that fish *real*?"

Mr. Roberts chuckled deeply. "Sure is. I caught that fellow myself. Pretty big, isn't he? Know much about salmon?" He gave Timothy a hearty pat on the back.

"No." Timothy caught his breath and shook his head.

"This is a king or Chinook salmon. They average 10 to 15 pounds, but it isn't unusual for them to weigh up to 126 pounds! And over

King Salmon

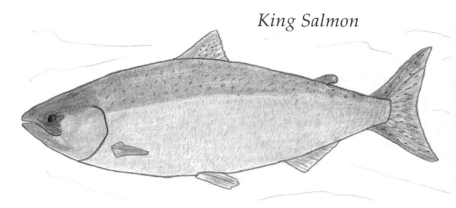

here on this wall is a silver or coho salmon. They are usually 6 to 10 pounds but can weigh up to 31 pounds."

"How do you tell a *big* silver and a *small* king salmon apart?" Timothy wondered.

"You look in their mouths," Mr. Roberts replied. "The king salmon's lower gums are all black, but the silver salmon has a white stripe at the base of his gums."

"And while I'm talking about fish, I want to

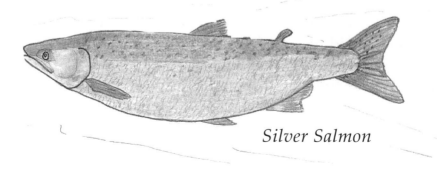

Silver Salmon

tell you about the strangest fish I ever caught."
Mr. Roberts loved to tell stories! "I reeled in
my line once, and a chubby puffin was on my
hook! He liked my bait too much. Thankfully,
he was unhurt, and I got to enjoy a close look
at him."

Mrs. Roberts perched comfortably in a worn
rocker. "Now you said you are moving, Elmer.
Why would you ever want to do that? You have
such a beautiful place there."

Uncle Elmer breathed a prayer for wisdom.
"Even though I had a lovely place, Hettie, I
wasn't happy inside. I knew I wasn't right with
the Lord of heaven and earth. Just a few weeks
ago, I repented of my sins and the Lord for-
gave me and cast my sins into the depths of the
sea. Now I want to move to be a part of a church
where they are doing what the Bible says. That
is why I'm moving."

Mr. Roberts rubbed his grizzly chin. "I've
seen plenty of church hypocrites in my day,"
he said thoughtfully. "But I can tell you folks
have something different."

"True, George." Mrs. Roberts nodded.
"Elmer, you look happier than you ever have
before. But come, let's take the children down
to see the tide pools and the cave. I'm sure they

Tufted puffin on fishing line

are tired of sitting." Although her hard gray eyes held a longing, she seemed only too glad to change the subject.

Soon they were strolling along a dirt road lined with tall trees. "Is that the ocean?" David wondered, getting a peek at the choppy water through the trees.

"No," Father replied with a smile, "that is the Strait of Juan de Fuca. The ocean water comes through it to the Hood Canal and Grandfather's beach."

"Isn't that Canada out there?" Joel wondered, looking at the mountainous land mass rising out of the strait in the distance. From their vantage point on the road at the top of the steep bank of the strait they had a panoramic view.

Mr. Roberts nodded. "Vancouver Island, British Columbia, to be exact."

"Look, I see One Dee again." David pointed to another glimpse of water through the trees.

"You mean Juan de Fuca?" Timothy asked with a grin.

"Yes." David nodded emphatically. "That Strait of One Dee!"

Timothy shrugged his shoulders helplessly as David skipped down the road, singing, "Dee!

Dee! One Dee! Dee! Dee! One Dee!"

"Stop and wait for us there, David," Father called. "That's far enough."

"And what a good place to stop," Mr. Roberts told David. "That's right where we want to go down. Watch your step, folks. It's steep in places here, but it's a lot easier than trying to slide down some of those rocky cliffs back there."

Once they were safely down on the rocky shore, Mr. Roberts led the way along the beach. "There are some small caves this way."

They followed their guide around and over rocks and across stretches of flat beach.

"Whew!" Uncle Elmer puffed. "You have an interesting trail. I see you are still in shape for getting around on these rocks."

Mr. Roberts grinned. "I've had lots of practice. And here we are." Mr. Roberts halted on a rock shelf in front of a shallow cave. A tall cliff rose above it. It was lined near the bottom with maidenhair ferns and red orange Indian paintbrush flowers.

"May we go into it?" Timothy wondered, eyeing the pile of boulders that filled most of the cave.

"I suppose," Father consented. "Those

boulders inside the cave look somewhat slippery though. I'll lead the way."

While the rest stood watching, Father and the older children climbed off the rock shelf they were standing on and plodded through the sand to the base of the rock pile. "Watch your step, children. Some of these boulders are slick."

Once she was at the top, Ruth looked around the cave. "I've seen about all I want to in here. May I go back to the others now, Father? There are some tide pools on the rock shelf that I would like to get a better look at."

He nodded.

Carefully, Ruth picked her way back down the rocky "path" and joined the others on the rock

Indian paintbrush

shelf. "Mother, what are these?" Ruth peered into the pool. "They look like green flowers, tipped with purple."

Mother walked over. "Those are sea anemones. Those 'petals' are their tentacles."

"Tentacles?" Ruth wrinkled her brow.

"Yes." Mother nodded. "Their tentacles contain stinging cells that paralyze the small marine

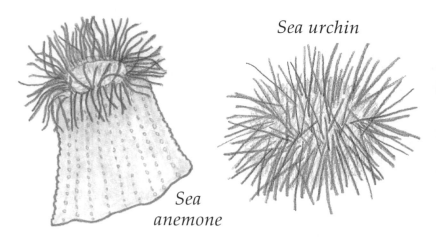

Sea urchin

Sea anemone

animals on which they prey."

"Are these other things pin cushions?" David wondered.

"Those are sea urchins," Grandmother told him. "Their 'pins' are spines that are set in ball-and-socket joints, somewhat like your arms."

Ruth laughed. "They look like round,

purple porcupines."

"What do?" Timothy scrambled onto the rock beside them.

"Sea urchins," replied Ruth with a smile.

Joel approached and gazed into the small tide pool. "Aren't they related to sea stars and sand dollars?"

"That's right," Mother affirmed. "I had forgotten that. God designed each of them to have groups of five or its multiple."

Timothy rolled up his sleeve and reached into the quiet pool. "He's stuck on well." He gently pried a prickly urchin off the rock.

"See?" He pointed to a pattern of five sets of tube feet on the flat, round underside. "Just like a starfish." He carefully placed it back into the water. "But, starfish have separate arms."

"O-o-o-oh! Look at this!" David had wandered to some nearby rocks overhanging another tide pool. "It's orange!"

"Why, you found a starfish." Father, who had joined them, came over to see. "That's a good-sized one."

Mr. Roberts glanced around for more. "Here's a purple one in this tide pool."

"Starfish are a very interesting part of God's creation," Uncle Elmer remarked. "They have a lot more feet than we do! Each of their tube feet is connected to a bulb of water surrounded by muscles. The muscles squeeze the bulb and force the water out to make the foot expand.

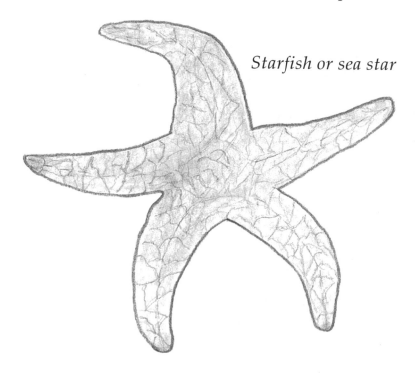

Starfish or sea star

Their feet stretch out and plant their suction cups and pull the body along. That's how they move."

"Back to sets of five," Father informed them, "Starfish have arms in sets of five, and each arm has an eye on the tip."

"Five eyes!" Timothy exclaimed.

"Yes, but they can't see," Uncle Elmer told him. "Their eyes are sensitive to light, but they have no vision."

"Hasn't God given them the ability to grow new arms?" Joel asked.

"Yes." Uncle Elmer touched the tiny, rough plates that made up the outer skeleton. "Their limbs duplicate exactly. Our Creator has put amazing properties in these sea creatures. Sometimes a whole new starfish will grow out of one arm and part of the center."

"Really?" Timothy scratched his head. "That *is* amazing!"

"This rock has a pointy bump!" David bent down for a closer look.

"Oh, that's a china men's hat." Grandfather bent down beside him. "Or a limpet."

"You mean it's alive?" David backed up.

Limpet

"Yes," said Grandfather, smiling. "There's a little animal under that cone-shaped shell."

"Oh! Will it bite?" David's eyes got wide.

"No, David, it won't

272

bite." Grandfather squeezed his shoulder. "It eats bits of food it scrapes off rocks."

He pulled out his pocketknife and slid the blade under the side of the one-inch cone. "See?" He held it out to David. "It has a soft, squishy body."

David took the tiny creature. He placed his finger on the suction cup bottom. "Oh, he's sticking to me! That feels funny."

After exploring a bit more, they headed back to the weather-beaten shack.

"I want to give you this before you go." Mr. Roberts pressed a bag into Father's hand. "It's smoked salmon. I didn't want you to visit our fishing town without getting some fish."

"Thank you," Father said with a smile. "I am sure we will enjoy it very much."

As they walked out to the car, Mr. Roberts walked beside Uncle Elmer. "Will you please pray for us?" he whispered. "You've given us a lot to think about today."

"I will," Uncle Elmer assured him. "I most certainly will. And I'll try to come back soon."

CHAPTER
TWENTY-FOUR

"Fire, and hail; snow, and vapours; stormy wind fulfilling his word."

Psalm 148:8

Himalayas and Hail

"Whew!" Timothy pushed back his straw hat and wiped the sweat from his brow. "August is a warm month." He jerked another weed out of the carrot patch.

"Yes," Ruth agreed. "But we don't have it as warm as they do in eastern Washington. It gets up to one hundred degrees there, while we seldom have it above ninety. And it's only eighty-six degrees today."

"You're right." Timothy tugged on a dandelion. "It could be a lot warmer."

"Timothy! Ruth! Please come!" Mother called from the house.

Leaving the weeds, they hurried to the house. "What, Mother?"

"Grandfather's Himalaya blackberries are ripe now. He wondered if we wanted to pick some today." She put some buckets on the table. "Fresh blackberry jam sounds good to me."

"It does." Timothy nodded. "I'm ready to pick." He twirled his hat on his fingers. "When do we start?"

"All right, then," Mother approved. "As soon as we can get ready, we'll go."

A cool breeze blew off the water at Grandfather's and fanned the hot berry pickers. "That wind feels good." Timothy carefully reached for a berry among the sharp prickles.

"Yes," Ruth agreed, plunking a handful of berries into her bucket.

"These are sweet." David popped a juicy blackberry into his mouth.

"They are bigger and sweeter than our little wild blackberries," Mother agreed.

"Ouch!" Timothy drew back his hand. "Their thorns are sharper too! I'm going to

David eating a green blackberry

have lots of scratches."

"Do try to be careful," Mother encouraged.

"I'm trying, but . . . " Timothy felt another poke on his purple finger. "But it's not always easy."

Ruth moved to another picking spot. "Blackberry jam will be worth it." She plucked a juicy berry from the thick, climbing vines.

"That isn't sweet." David bit into a hard green berry. "Green ones don't taste good."

Timothy grinned. "You should only eat the black ones. The green and red berries aren't ready to eat yet."

"I know that now." David hurriedly ate a few ripe berries to rid himself of the tart taste. "No green berries for me!"

A few hours later, Mother smiled, observing the full buckets of berries. "Grandfather's patch was full of berries, wasn't it? This should make lots of jelly."

"You knew just when to pick them, Grandfather," Ruth commended.

He smiled. "After so many years of berry picking, you can tell when they are at the peak of the season. I'm glad you came today. Soon the rains will return, and all the ripe berries will spoil quickly."

Himalaya blackberry

Himalayas and Hail

"Maybe they are coming now." Timothy eyed a huge thunderhead casting a shadow on the foothills of the Olympic Mountains across the Hood Canal.

"Maybe," Grandfather admitted. "But our drizzles often wait to increase until September or October. July and August are our warmest months."

"Why don't you come in out of the sun?" Grandmother offered. "We can help you clean these while you rest and have a glass of lemonade."

"That does sound good." Mother picked up two of the pails heaped with plump, ripe fruit. "But there is no need for you to help us clean these. I have some good helpers." She smiled at the children.

"Well, we can help you get started." Grandfather helped carry the rest of the berries into the house.

Bang! Bang! Bang!

David set his lemonade down and scurried to the window. "Oh! Oh! It's snowing!"

Mother looked up from the berries she was sorting. "I think it is hailing, David."

Everyone dropped what they were doing and hurried to the window. "Look at them

281

bounce." Timothy watched the hailstones hit the walk below.

"What is it called?" David turned to Mother.

"Hail."

"Hail," he repeated. "Hail. Hail. Hail. Hopping hail. Hop. Hop! Hop!" He started jumping around.

"Just like you." Timothy grinned.

Mother put her hand on David's shoulder. "That's enough, son. You may hop like hail outside, but not inside."

"All right," he said meekly as he walked back to the window.

The pounding suddenly slowed, and David frowned. "It's going away."

"Hailstorms usually don't last very long." Grandfather looked out over the white-speckled lawn. "I'd say this berry picking was the Lord's timing, wouldn't you?"

"God was good." Mother nodded. "If we had waited another day, the berries would have been pelted by hail."

Knock. Knock. Knock-knock.

"Now that's a familiar pounding," Grandfather said with a smile. "Come in, Elmer!"

Uncle Elmer slipped in the door and dropped his hat onto the coat rack. "That was a quick storm. Looks like I'm a little late for picking berries."

"I'll make some jam for you," Mother offered. "I'll be glad to."

"Well, I'd appreciate that," Uncle Elmer said gratefully. "I think the hail took care of any berries that were left."

"How does God make hail?" Ruth wondered.

"Hail is made of frozen water droplets formed high in the clouds," Grandfather began. "The hailstones get tossed up and down in the thunderhead. They collect water droplets in the lower part of the cloud and get blown back into the upper part, where ice crystals stick to their wet surface and freeze. When they get too heavy, they fall."

Ruth nodded. "Just like rain, because of gravity."

"If you cut them in the middle, they would look like an onion." Uncle Elmer smiled. "They may have several layers of ice."

"We usually have small hailstones," Grandfather told them. "But in Kansas, one was reported that was almost the size of a man's head. It was as heavy as a melon."

Timothy's eyes widened. "Now that's big!"

"'Hast thou seen the treasures of the hail . . . ?'" Uncle Elmer quoted. "We have a great Creator who does great things."

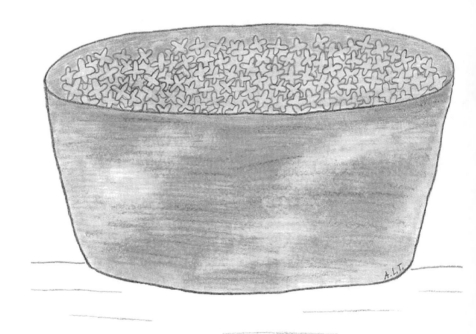

CHAPTER
TWENTY-FIVE

"The eyes of all wait upon thee: and thou givest them their meat in due season. Thou openest thine hand, and satisfiest the desire of every living thing. The Lord is righteous in all his ways, and holy in all his works."

Psalm 145:15–17

Cat Food Thieves

Meow. The call broke the stillness of the crisp September day.

Ruth looked up from the cookies she was dropping onto the cookie sheet. "Did you hear that meow, Mother? It didn't sound like Spice."

"It didn't, but you should check anyway," Mother told her. "Maybe Spice needs more food."

As Ruth opened the door, a blue-and-black

jay flew to a nearby hemlock tree. "There's no cat out here. Just a Steller's jay."

Jay! Jay! the bird scolded her.

"Aren't you noisy?" Ruth laughed as she closed the door.

"Does Spice still have food?" Mother wondered.

"Yes." Ruth placed the cookie sheet into the oven. "But I didn't see a cat. That's strange."

Meow.

Ruth crept over to the door.

The jay swooped from the hemlock onto the deck rail. Hop. Hop. Hop. He was soon near the door. *Meow.* He cocked his head and jumped down to snatch a piece of cat food.

"Mother!" Ruth gasped. "The Steller's jay said 'meow'!"

"He did?" Mother quietly hurried over.

The beautiful royal blue bird raised his black crest and looked at them with his beady black eyes before taking another piece. *Meow.*

"He copies Spice and eats her food!" Ruth watched him fly back to the hemlock. "What a bird!"

"I knew jays could imitate hawks." Mother went back to her baking. "But I didn't know they could imitate cats too."

Steller's jay

Jay! Jay! he scolded.

Ruth went for her bird book. "It says they are excellent mimics and can imitate crows and loons, besides hawks."

"They are bold birds." Mother saw him land on the railing again. "And they eat almost anything."

"Including Spice's food!" Ruth glanced at the jay as he gobbled another piece.

Darkness was settling in earlier and earlier as fall approached. "Sorry supper is so late," Mother apologized as she set the steaming casserole on the table that evening. "We were so busy baking that the oven was occupied when it was time to put supper in."

"That is all right," Father assured her. "I was late also. At least we know everyone is hungry."

"I know I am." Timothy took his seat.

After prayer, Mother began dishing up the casserole.

Bang! Boom! A crash sounded from the deck on the back of the house.

Joel and Timothy jumped up quickly. "Please excuse us."

Joel flipped on the light and peered out in time to see a retreating gray figure. "Whatever it was, it wasn't Spice."

"Leave the light on," Father instructed. "It may be back. You can eat while you're waiting."

Timothy took another bite of beef casserole. "This is good, Mother."

"Thank you," Mother replied. "I hope it was worth waiting for."

"It was." Timothy sat up straighter and listened carefully. "I think I hear something."

David pushed his chair back. "I want to see."

"Wait, David." Father held him back. "Let Timothy check first."

Timothy crept over to the door and peeked out. "Oh." Two pairs of eyes met his. "Raccoons!"

"Quietly, everyone." Father slowly pushed his chair back.

Soon the whole family was clustered at the back door. A wary coon hastily grabbed a handful of cat food with both paws and gobbled it down.

"He keeps looking at us," Ruth whispered.

A second coon stood watching. "That one is smaller," Joel noticed.

Another masked face peeked over the edge of the deck and scrambled up. "It must be a mother and her babies," Timothy rightly concluded.

Raccoons

"They look plump enough," Joel observed.

"What else do they eat?" Timothy wondered.

"I know they eat crayfish and . . . and cat food," Joel replied. "But I'll have to look it up."

"They ate every bit of Spice's food!" Ruth watched them disappear over the deck edge and vanish into the night. "That is why her dish is almost always empty in the morning! Poor Spice. I didn't think she could eat that much food every day. See, Timothy, she wasn't so greedy after all."

But Timothy had disappeared around the corner. "Here it is," he called. "This book tells about raccoons."

"What does it say they eat?" Ruth asked.

"Fruit, nuts, grains, insects, frogs, fish, crayfish, bird's eggs," he listed. "And Spice's food," he added in fun. "At least that's what I say!"

"You have an animal feeder right by the back door, Ruth," Mother said.

"I should say so!" She laughed. "We had two kinds of visitors at Spice's dish already today."

CHAPTER
TWENTY-SIX

"Nevertheless he left not himself without witness, in that he did good, and gave us rain from heaven, and fruitful seasons, filling our hearts with food and gladness."
Acts 14:17

Fall Returns

Chick-a-dee-dee-dee.

Ruth dropped another handful of shiny blackish blue berries into her bucket. "There's a flock of small birds coming. Please be quiet, Timothy." She stood very still as they came closer.

A small olive gray bird landed on a branch next to her. *Tee. Tee. Tee,* it peeped softly, flicking its wings.

"What a sweet little bird!" she exclaimed quietly.

His tiny black eye focused on Ruth. Tilting his head, he fluttered to another branch.

"Oh, he has a shiny red patch on the top of his head." She caught a glimpse of it. "What could he be?"

Just then another plump little bird landed on a nearby fence post, looking at Ruth with inquisitive eyes. "Why, it is like the other one, except that it has yellow, black, and white stripes on its head instead of a red patch."

Chick-a-dee-dee. Another bird sang from overhead.

Ruth glanced up to see him hanging upside down from a Douglas fir branch. "That chickadee has chestnut brown on his back. I'm going to have to look these birds up in my bird book. I haven't seen them before."

The nearby trees seemed full of the friendly little birds. *Tee. Tee. Tee. Chick-a-dee-dee-dee.* The songs grew fainter as the birds flew on in their search for food.

"Did you see them, Timothy?" She turned to her brother.

Timothy resumed his berry picking. "Yes. They were cheerful little birds, weren't they?"

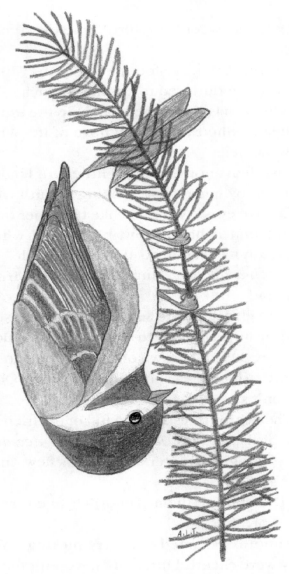

Chestnut-backed chickadee

"I want to look them up." Ruth tilted her hand and rolled more dark blue berries into her bucket. "I don't remember seeing them before."

"It sure takes a while to pick these huckleberries," Timothy remarked. "They are even smaller than our red huckleberries."

Ruth stroked a small, shiny leaf. "I'm about done with this bush. Shall we go down to the patch by the road?"

"Okay," Timothy agreed. "Let's get Joel first. Father didn't need him at work today, and Mother would want him along when we are down by the road."

Soon the trio was strolling down the lane, laden with berry buckets. "This is the trail to the patch, isn't it?" Joel plunged into the underbrush. "Hasn't been used for a while. And here we are." Joel broke into a small clearing and paused as Timothy and Ruth trudged through the brush behind him.

"Ouch." Ruth rubbed her cheek where a branch snapped back and hit her. "I forgot that I shouldn't follow you so closely, Timothy! You are plowing through the brush like a bear."

"Sorry, sis." Timothy apologized, but grinned at her description. "I'll try to be more careful. Guess I can't keep up with Joel, even if I do make enough commotion for a bear!"

Though the small patch was near the road, the underbrush formed walls on all sides of the little clearing. Time slipped away while the three busily applied themselves to picking berries.

Joel ran his fingers over a leaf that had a

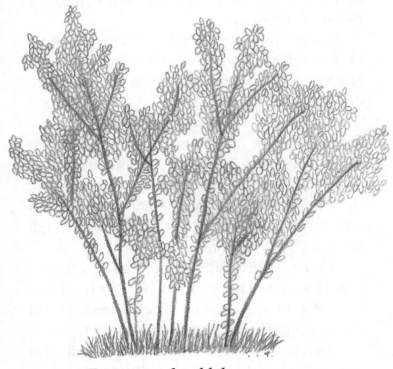

Evergreen huckleberry

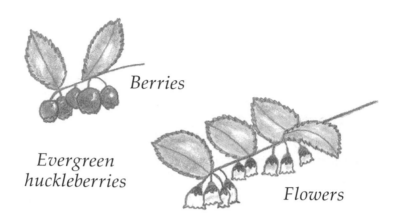

Berries

*Evergreen
huckleberries*

Flowers

fine-toothed margin. "Did you know this is our
only evergreen huckleberry?"

"No, I didn't." Ruth moved to another bush.

"All our other huckleberries lose their
leaves, just like the red ones do."

"Yes, that's right." A familiar voice made
Ruth jump.

"Uncle Elmer! I didn't know you were here."

Uncle Elmer chuckled as he stepped into
the small clearing.

Father came out from the bushes behind
him. "Didn't you remember I was bringing a
guest home for supper tonight?"

Joel smiled. "That's right. I'm glad you could
come, Uncle Elmer."

"These make good pies," Timothy remarked,

filling his hand with berries. "But it seems I'm not picking them very fast."

"Well, keep at it, and we'll give you a hand," Father offered, and he and Uncle Elmer started picking.

Joel grinned. "We'll be done soon with all this help. I'm surprised we didn't hear you coming."

"You must have been absorbed in your task," Uncle Elmer said.

"And you don't make as much noise as I do," Timothy chuckled.

A strong breeze whipped past the berry pickers and swayed the treetops. Ruth glanced up at the overcast sky. "We'd better be done soon, or we might get wet."

Darkness had enveloped the brown house in the clearing. Rain pattered on the windows as the wind whipped the drops against the house. "Fall is here again." Joel stood by the window and in the glow of the outdoor light watched the drops fall.

Ruth sorted through a handful of berries, picking out the stems. "I'm thankful the Lord gave us enough time to pick these before the rain started. And thank you for helping us, Uncle Elmer."

"It was my pleasure," he replied. "Your mother's huckleberry pie was a good reward for all our efforts."

"Yes." Timothy grabbed a handful to sort. "That was delicious, Mother. Oh, Ruth, did you ever look up those birds that we saw?"

"No, I didn't," Ruth replied, pouring her handful of sorted berries in with the other clean ones. "If it is all right with you, Mother, I'll go do that now."

At Mother's nod, she went to get her bird book. "Here are the chickadees. The one we saw must have been a chestnut-backed chickadee. It says they are common here."

"What were those olive gray ones?" Timothy wondered.

"That's what I'm going to look for now." Ruth flipped through the book, glancing at each page. "I'm curious to know—oh, here they are. They were kinglets."

"Kinglets?" Timothy dropped his handful of berries and came over to see.

"It says they are our smallest birds except for the hummingbirds," Ruth was reading.

"They looked fairly small," Timothy stated as he studied the drawings. "Didn't we see both kinds?"

Golden-crowned kinglet

Ruby-
crowned
kinglet

"Yes, we did." Ruth nodded. "A male ruby-crowned kinglet landed right beside me. His small red head patch looked just like a hummingbird's chin feathers."

"A golden crowned kinglet was visiting me." Timothy pointed to the picture. "He almost landed on my head!"

"It says here that they're friendly. Why haven't I seen them before?" Ruth wondered.

Mother came over to the pair as a fresh gust of wind sent the raindrops splattering against the windowpane. "I've seen those birds before. At least once a week a flock goes by in the trees outside the kitchen window."

"Really?" Ruth looked surprised. "Where have I been?"

"Catching butterflies?" Joel teased.

As Father dropped the last handful of sorted berries into the bowl, Uncle Elmer said, "I have some wonderful news I want to share with you tonight. Just today I got a letter from George Roberts, and they have both given their lives to the Lord."

"Praise God," Father said fervently.

"And they are looking for a Scriptural church now," Uncle Elmer supplied. "I think they would like to come visit here soon. I am so thankful we went to see them before I moved."

David beamed. "That means three people we prayed for know God now. I am so happy!"

"And so am I." Uncle Elmer's eyes shone.

A jagged streak of lightning pierced the darkness, and the thunder boomed in reply.

Ruth shivered. "I'm glad I'm not out there."

"It is rather stormy, isn't it?" Joel walked over to the window. "The October rainstorms have returned."

"I enjoy the different seasons," Ruth sighed. "I even like our rainstorms."

"I know I do," Timothy put in. "Maybe the power will go out and we can cook on the wood stove. That's one of the exciting things about fall storms."

Uncle Elmer joined Joel at the window. "You know, each change in the seasons reminds me of the promise of God. As long as the earth stands, summer and winter, springtime and harvest will not cease. What a great Creator we serve! Each part of His Creation has special design!"

"Oh that men would praise the Lord for his goodness, and for his wonderful works to the children of men!" (Psalm 107:15).